THE COSMIC
INTERNET

"Frank DeMarco's book, *The Cosmic Internet,* offers an exceptionally lucid and informative voice. Who are we? Why are we here? What is the nature of healing? What about guidance? All these questions are treated and so many more! This is a contact the seeker will find full of resources. Buy this book!"
—Carla Rueckert-McCarthy, author of *The Law of One*

"Fifty years from now a new generation will wonder why this was such a ground-breaking book. They will be astounded that all this information had to be introduced and explained in *The Cosmic Internet.*
—Charles Sides, author of *Motorcycle Enlightenment*

"If this is mysticism, it's a singularly practical mysticism."
—Michael Ventura, author of *The Zoo Where You're Fed to God*

Books by Frank DeMarco

Fiction

Messenger: A Sequel to Lost Horizon
Babe in the Woods

Non-fiction

Muddy Tracks: Exploring an Unsuspected Reality
Chasing Smallwood: Talking with the Other Side
The Sphere and the Hologram: Explanations from the Other Side

THE COSMIC
INTERNET

EXPLANATIONS FROM THE OTHER SIDE

FRANK DeMARCO

Author of *Muddy Tracks*

RAINBOW RIDGE
BOOKS

Cover and Interior design by Frame25 Productions
Cover Photo © argus c/o Shutterstock.com

Published by:
Rainbow Ridge Books, LLC
140 Rainbow Ridge Road
Faber, Virginia 22938
434-361-1723

If you are unable to order this book from your local
bookseller, you may order directly from the distributor.

Square One Publishers, Inc.
115 Herricks Road
Garden City Park, NY 11040
Phone: (516) 535-2010
Fax: (516) 535-2014
Toll-free: 877-900-BOOK

Visit the author at:
www.hologrambooks.com

Library of Congress Cataloging-in-Publication Data applied for.

ISBN 978-0-9844955-4-2

10 9 8 7 6 5 4 3 2

Printed on acid-free paper in the United States

To my cherished friends and fellow explorers, especially

Nancy Ford
Absolutely straight

Michael Peter Langevin
Shaman, pirate, magician

Acknowledgements

ROBERT S. FRIEDMAN—Bob—saw the value of the material from the first and encouraged me to turn it into a book. Bob has been publishing consciousness-raising books for 35 years, first as co-founder of The Donning Company, then as co-founder of Hampton Roads Publishing Company, and he continues today with his Rainbow Ridge line with Square One books. And here we are (as Carlyle once said to Emerson) shoveled together again.

Analytical Table of Contents

Introduction   xi

Chapter One: A Model of Our Minds on the Other Side   1

Contradictory Story • Religious Understandings • The Spiritual Problem Of Western Civilization • Old Models Of Consciousness The Physical And The Non-Physical • Minds On The Other Side Influences On The Individual • Redefining Ourselves And The World Life as Preparation • Grounding The Model

Chapter Two: The Individual as Convenient Fiction   33

The Complicated Human Existence • Why Convenient, Why Fiction Rings And Threads • Mind As Habit • A Unique Collection Of Threads • Understanding Threads • Genetic Heredity • The Software of the Individual • Spiritual Heredity • Works In Progress • Many Lives Within A Life • Vertical Integration • As Above, So Below Three Levels

Chapter Three: The Physical and the Non-Physical   69

Why Does The World Exist? • Space, Time, And The Illusion Of Separation • Creation And Creator • A Continuing Interaction Only One Thing Exists • Spiritual Influences On The Consciousness New Understandings • Three Eras, Three Views Of Reality • Souls, Traits And Reincarnation • Significantly Different Lives • A Matter Of Definition • Past-Life Memory • Fluctuating Consciousness • The Porous Nature Of Consciousness • More On The Porous Nature Of Consciousness • Continual Internal Interaction

Chapter Four: Living Connected   133

Communication Across The Veil • The Conscious And Unconscious Minds • A Tangled Question • Using Guidance • Deepening Access Consciousness As Movement • Our Work • Complementary Advantages • Our Lives As Ringmasters • Two Ways Of Connecting Perception And Morality • You Shall Be Your Own Interpreters TGU As The Expression Of Forces • Guidance, Suffering And The Virtues • The Limits To Intuition • Accident And Necessity • Our Situation As Individuals • Humility And Gratitude

Chapter Five: Shaping Your Life   181

Ships • Living Close To The Unconscious • Wholeness • Life Amid Polarities • Discouragement, Its Causes And Cure • Awakening • Three Simple Techniques • 1) Reprogramming • 2) Guidance • 3) Visualizations Staying Connected

Conclusion   209

Introduction

"It is not that I have accomplished too few of my plans, for I am not ambitious. But when I think of all the books I have read, and of the wise words I have heard spoken, and of the anxiety I have given to parents and grandparents, and of the hopes that I have had, all life weighed in the scales of my own life seems to me a preparation for something that never happens."
—W.B. Yeats, *Autobiographies*, page 106.

LIFE SEEMS TO TAKE a long time while it is passing, but at a certain age you look back and realize that you've already had most of the time you're likely to have on this earth. You think: What did I accomplish? What was it all about? Where is the meaning in any of it? When I was young, I'd look at famous people who had achieved things, and I'd wonder how they felt when they knew they were dying. Even more than that, I'd think of how we all—famous or unknown—spend our lives learning things, accumulating skills and experiences, constructing inner worlds that could never be translated to anyone else. I'd think, "all that work, all those connections made, all those books read and associated one with another, all that time invested in people—in anything the person loved—all gone, the moment they die." I was all but paralyzed by the pointlessness of achieving or learning or even experiencing anything. If it all crumbles as soon as we do—what's the use?

Obviously this doesn't strike everyone the same way. Some people don't seem to notice, or they don't think about it. Others, having abandoned hope of physical immortality, work to "leave the world a better place," or seek to leave an immortal name through achievement. Others concentrate on actively enjoying every moment. Still others hope for eternal life in paradise—and even this makes anything we do or strive to do on earth, other than being "good" in order to be "saved," irrelevant.

None of these ways of experiencing life gave any indication that our lives were meaningful. None of them seemed to *connect* with how we actually live our lives. The afterlife in scriptures remained a vague idea, at best nothing one could grasp, at worst perhaps merely a threat and a promise designed to keep people in line. But life without an afterlife, as postulated by materialists, made even less sense of life.

But if neither the believers nor the materialists provide us with a credible picture of the meaning and nature of life, where could we find one? Ideally, we would go right to the source, communicating directly with the other side of life, the non-physical side. Direct communication would be as close to first-hand information as we could get until we ourselves drop the body and cross over. Interestingly, some people insisted that this is possible.

So the question became, *is* it possible? And if possible, is it safe? And if both possible and safe, could we trust anyone and everyone we might contact on the other side?

These questions aren't new. They have been asked and answered for as long as people have been aware that material life is only half the picture. The answers have come in different forms, shaped to the needs of different peoples, different civilizations. Any culture's scriptures deal with interaction between the physical and the non-physical aspects of the world. The problems, the techniques, the models are, after all, just so many varieties of packaging. Old words go dead on new generations, and so old truths have to be restated to be heard. The reality is the same.

Over the past five years, communicating with certain minds in the non-physical world, I have gotten information that amounts to an intellectually respectable model that makes sense of our lives in the physical and non-physical world. I've gotten it over time, in bits and pieces, but they've left it up to me to put together the pieces as best I could (no doubt, with their behind-the-scenes prodding). This book is my attempt to do just that.

The way I communicate is shaped by who I am and how I came to the work. I offer you my experience because, as a modern version of the ancient quest, it may seem less strange to you than previous offerings. But of course, I am aware that with every tick of the clock, my experience recedes and becomes less current. That doesn't matter. The future will have its own testimonies. The important thing is not that the message be chiseled in stone, but that it be delivered.

It's a good message, and hopeful. When we realize that we do *not* cease to exist when we drop the body, that the mind that we shape continues to function and may be used more surely and accurately and accessibly than ever, then not only was nothing lost, much was gained. And in the meantime, while we are still living in the physical world, non-physical beings are here for us. It is merely a matter of learning how to communicate with them.

2.

The family and the religious tradition I was born into had nothing to do with talking to spirits. I was born in 1946, less than a year after the end of World War II, into a family of Catholic Italian-Americans. My father was easy-going and skeptical, my mother orthodox and devout. I began devout, became skeptical, and left the church in my teens, unable and unwilling to live within its rules and restrictions. But I had been shaped more than I knew by growing up in a tradition that took for granted that this physical world was underpinned by an invisible reality that was primary, rather than secondary. My spiritually formative years had been spent in the Catholic Church as it existed in postwar America. So, I grew up with one foot in bustling, confident postwar America and the other in almost a medieval worldview.

In my college years I read Jess Stearn's *The Sleeping Prophet* and Thomas Sugrue's *There is a River*, which told of Edgar Cayce's trance channeling sessions from the 1920s through the mid-1940s, captured in shorthand, typed up, and filed in the archives of his Association for Research and Enlightenment. Those sessions contained remarkable and well-attested prescriptions that led to the healing of many whom conventional medicine could not help. They talked of past-life connections, paths to spiritual development, and dire prophecies of our future if we did not change our ways. I believed what I read, but it didn't occur to me that others could learn to do what he did. It would be a good long time before it occurred to me that Jesus had said that others would do what he had done, and would in fact do even greater things. As a boy I assumed that this referred to "special" people like his disciples. It didn't occur to me that he might mean me, and you.

Cayce served as an entry point into the strange world of the occult, as it was then called. But what a labyrinth *that* proved to be! I spent years searching through books filled with assertions, looking for something clear and authoritative. Instead I found chaos—often pretentious chaos. I was never tempted to follow gurus, and was unable to bring myself to join any of the societies I learned of. So many sects, each proclaiming that it, and presumably *only* it, had the truth. Where was the key? Where were the undisputed facts?

Having left the spiritual tradition I had grown up in, the

only tool I had to work with was my intuition. This put me in the position of having to decide, before examination, whether something was worth examining, which is absurd. Nonetheless, this is the fix I was in, and am in still. I still don't know any other way for us to proceed but to keep discarding what we cannot use, and keep looking for what is food and drink to us. You can't necessarily depend on the judgment and experience of others, for "one man's meat is another man's poison." Your soul, like your body, will react to poison when it experiences it, and it is up to you to recognize the reaction and reject the poison. But you'd better hope that you recognize it as poison before you've eaten too much of it!

The more first-hand experience I got of dealing with what I call "the other side," the more I could see that it harmonized with *a certain way* of looking at Catholic doctrine. On the other hand, the conclusions I drew from it didn't necessarily agree with the church's conclusions. So I was left relying on the inner knowing that is our birthright, that intuitive sense that "this is the way for me, regardless whether it is the way for others." In short, I was still on my own.

At first, when I explored reincarnation and past lives, naturally I was thinking of those subjects the way most people seem to do. But with time and experience it became clear that our explorations are hampered by careless assumptions and bad definitions. We assume that reincarnation is a matter of one person moving from one life to another. We assume that we in this life are separate from those other lives. We assume that even if *they* influence *us*, *we* do not influence *them*. My experience argues that none of these assumptions are correct.

"But"—you ought to be objecting—"these are old, old subjects. What makes you an expert on the basis of a few years' experience?" If I were relying on my own personal resources, I wouldn't have much worthwhile to say. But much of the information and most of the concepts contained here came via altered-state experiences, alone or with others. That gives access to a tremendous amount of knowledge, wisdom and experience.

When the breakthrough came, it didn't take place out of thin air. I had been preparing myself for it—unknowingly—for years, as I described in my 2001 book *Muddy Tracks*. Then I and my friend Rita Warren began a long series of weekly sessions with the guys upstairs. Rita was a Ph.D. psychologist with decades of experience both in the academic world and in the world of psychic investigation. (She had run Bob Monroe's consciousness lab at The Monroe Institute for four years before re-retiring.) Her years of working with people in altered states had given her a list of unanswered questions about life on the other side. In 22 sessions over five months, she asked these questions of the guys upstairs, and they talked, and explained, and answered more questions, and drew analogies, and answered her supplementary questions based on their answers in prior sessions. As Rita and I began to absorb the answers, we gradually realized that this new way of viewing things was changing the way we lived our lives. We came to be living in a new world, with much greater assurance that it's true, what the guys continually told us, that "all is well; all is always well."

I published the transcripts of these sessions in 2009 as *The Sphere and the Hologram*, about a year after Rita made her transition into the non-physical. By that time, my connections with disembodied intelligences had broadened and deepened considerably. Beginning in late 2005, I had the great good fortune to experience six months of daily written conversations first with a "past life" and then with various authors and historical figures. I published an account of the first part of that process, also in 2009, as *Chasing Smallwood*. So here I am in my sixties, talking to non-physical people. Some have been dead a few years, some for decades, or centuries. Apparently I may talk to nearly anyone I wish to, provided that I have a real reason to do so. I seem to have tapped into the invisible world's Internet.

Much of this material came in early-morning sessions. I

would sit with my journal and write out questions, or merely announce that I was open for business, and then I would write out what came. Bear in mind, it isn't as if I was actually physically hearing words, nor did I usually hear the words in my head. Mostly it happened the way it does when you sit down to write a letter. You start a sentence and you don't necessarily know how the sentence is going to end, or what it is going to lead to next. You start, and the words well up from somewhere, and as you write them, more well up.

Sometimes what came had the flavor of a prepared talk. Sometimes it became a dialogue, often enough with us bantering back and forth. Sometimes I was taking dictation and sometimes it was as if I was overhearing them talking to themselves, thinking aloud, and sometimes I would have a sense of what they wanted to communicate but would have to find the words myself. It was always entertaining, with a flavor much like the continuing dialogues we have via the Internet, talking with unseen friends at a distance. In fact, that isn't a bad model for the relationship—friends interacting at a distance. In my original experiments, more than 20 years ago, I thought I was talking to my anima, whom I arbitrarily named Evangeline and thought of, humorously, as The Boss. Then came various individual "past lives," then the concept of TGU, then Jung and Lincoln and other historical figures.

Unlike Jane Roberts' Seth, who dictated sentences and paragraphs and specified titles and chapter headings, my contacts (who I usually just called "the guys upstairs," or TGU) left it to me to find a way to make these things accessible to others, and it took a long, long time to figure out how to do so. I give you the conversations as I transcribed and edited them, where necessary adding bridging remarks *[set off in brackets and italics, like this]*. In places where I and they interact, my sentences are always in *italics*. I should add that the entries, which were received between 2006 and 2010, are not in sequence. Therefore I have omitted dating any of the entries, lest dating add confusion.

Below, an example, a conversation with Swiss psychologist Carl Jung, or a spirit claiming to be Carl Jung, or my own imagining of what Carl Jung would have to say, or—. You see the problem. I have enormous respect for Jung, and it was almost too much for me to accept that he was choosing me as a means (not necessarily the *only* means) through which he could address the world. Perhaps it is as big a step for you. If so, I suggest that you join me in paying attention to what is said, rather than worrying too much about whether in fact he is the source.

Carl Jung on Exploring

Dr. Jung, can you provide some context for what is going on here? I'm beyond suspecting that I am "making this up" except that the more I think about it the less I have any idea what's really going on, how I should really be looking at all this. I'm not really simple enough to take all this at its face value either as legitimate contact or as construct of my own mind.

You are in deep waters, and you prefer to be able to stand firmly on the bottom. And yet you want to go sailing. Very well, if you wish to sail and you cannot swim, it is well for you to not fall out of the boat, or else go sailing wearing always a life preserver! But life preservers are not much fun, so you must learn to swim, or be sure to not fall out of the boat, or stay ashore.

And you do not quite know how to swim—although, you float quite vigorously!—and so you are confined to your boat and in fact are confined a bit in what you dare do in your boat lest you fall off. But enough of analogy. "Your boat" really refers to the concepts you use in order to make sense of your experiences. This is necessary if you are to sail farther and acquire even newer experiences. Otherwise you are swimming alone and the strangeness could overwhelm you.

Your question is, what is going on? Who are you talking to?

What is the process? You have a working hypothesis. Why do you feel the need to abandon it or modify it, and why use me rather than yourself?

Well surely it is obvious. I don't know if my explanation is right—and how can I find out by asking part of the manifestation if it is what it seems to be?

Precisely. So—nevertheless you ask. Having called spirits from the vasty deep you ask them if they are really spirits, and if they are really from the vasty deep, or if you are making the whole thing up.

And it's ridiculous, I know. It is exactly like asking somebody if they exist outside of my own mind. In the nature of things, the answer is inside the frame of reference. I don't suppose we could ever really prove that anybody *else exists, really—because all the evidence that* seems *to be sensory has been processed by our own mind.*

And so you should ask yourself, why does this question remain important to you? Regardless what the *answer* is, the fact that you are presented with is that the *question* exists and is real for you and important.

And for someone else, it might not be.

That's right. Your questions define you much more than your answers do.

I have been working on the assumption that this experience is for the sake of others, not just for me. The fact that I am willing to experiment in public is—I take it—one of my qualifications for the job. Well, if this is true, setting out my doubts and problems is a good thing, surely, so as to encourage others to begin or continue. But it seems to me that some tentative structure is equally important.

Yes, but anyone doing something by following another person's example has a pitfall to deal with that the first person does not. The very fact that you have recorded your experiments makes them more real, more objective. It gives them greater weight, to the person reading of them or hearing of them. It tempts followers to assume that you know more, can do more, *are* more, than they. It can scarcely be avoided. Perhaps it *shouldn't* be avoided, for in its own way it can be an encouragement. But wrongly used—or rather, revered instead of being used—it becomes a pitfall. When you read of another's efforts and you sympathize with them, there is a temptation to set the experimenter higher than yourself in your estimation. Were you not told that too much admiration sets a distance between people that hampers communication?

Yes. I see. So do you think it would be a bad thing, or say a useless thing, to try to make a structure to contain this in?

Why should you wish to *contain* it? To contain it is to confine the ship to the harbor. You know the saying about ships and harbors.

Yes I do. Ships are safe in harbors but that isn't what ships are made for.

So?

So how about if we at least sketch out the structure of the ship itself?

To reassure the sailors, presumably.

Well, sure, I guess that's what it amounts to.

Very well, look at it this way. You are a consciousness, a part of which is confined within a body and the body's experiences.

To the degree that you restrict your awareness to that part of your consciousness only, you will live in a world of senses and, perhaps, thoughts. But that world will be haunted by dreams and the irrational. Things will occur that are seemingly external to you, seeded from chaos. Life may become a struggle for sanity.

Religions were created for many reasons, not least of which to provide a formal social acknowledgement that the consciousness of the senses is not the end of the story. The idea, you see, is just what you were proposing—by giving people a framework, perhaps they would feel more comfortable, exploring. But not everyone needs religion for that purpose. Some find their consciousness ranging far and wide beyond the body, and some find this exhilarating and some find it frightening and some don't think much about it, taking it as natural. In this difference in reaction you may see a difference in types, as I studied long ago.

In a time in which religion is alive to people, anyone's imaginings, dreams, experiences, visitations, apparitions, communications, are fitted into the framework the religion provides, and thus they make sense, pretty easily. These are not the kind of times you live in—or wish to live in, or you would be living in other times! In your times, the old religion—the old way of linking up, which is what the word religion means—has lost its vitality. New myths, new containers, are being shaped, as you live through the process. Your great-grandchildren will live within a new myth that more closely matches their psychic reality. There is nothing wrong with the process, neither the making of myths nor the outgrowing of myths. How else is chaos to be contained, save in form? How else is growth to occur, save in the breaking of form?

Living as you do—as I did, but in an earlier phase of it—in which the old gods have left the forms that society had become accustomed to, you have a transitory freedom of exploration that has its advantages and disadvantages.,

No one can see God's unshielded face, religious tradition tells us. What does this mean? One meaning is simply that the created cannot comprehend that which created it. Another meaning is that the consciousness, while confined within form, cannot comprehend the formless, but immediately and inevitably attempts to confine the formless in some sort of definition that consciousness-within-form can grasp. You know the Sufi saying. It is very true: "Words are a prison. God is free."

Well, if you cannot *really* see the infinite as it is—not from want of will or want of intensity or want of depth or want of sustained effort but in the nature of things—then you must resign yourself to the knowledge that whatever glimpse you get is precious, but incomplete; infinitely valuable, but misunderstood and not very communicable. In times between eras, times between myths, times between religions, in times when the gods have left their former habitations and have not yet had new houses built for them by man—in your time, in other words—you can *see* this inability to comprehend the infinite. The times between gods (if you care to look at it that way) allow people to see between the cracks and remember how little we ever see. Later, when we are worshipping the gods in these new houses, we will find it easier to forget that still we do not see them face to face.

This should serve as a reminder that the fact that you do not *know* is actually a good thing, for it merely means that for the moment you are awake to a reality that persists but is forgotten. *You can never know* at any absolute level. Given that you cannot know if pink looks to your neighbor as it does to you, can you expect to compare visions of the formless? There is no harm, and much use, in making such comparisons provided that you remember the limits to your certainties. But it is precisely this remembering that you will find very hard to do. The continual recurring temptation will be to fall into certainty or to cease to explore.

3.

So there is an example of the kind of material I have been bringing through. What, if anything, it means to your life is for you to decide. The only guarantee I can offer is that I am not deliberately deceiving you. Whether what you hear is true, and whether the source is as claimed, is for you to discern.

Isn't the first question how it can be possible? This is where experience is superior to theory. When we have experienced certain things, we don't have to speculate as to whether those things are possible. Experience gives us grounding in a way that theory cannot. So, here, based on that experience, I propose to answer certain questions. Among others: How can dead people talk with us, and talk to each other—regardless when they lived—and talk about *our* time, which was *their* future? How can they be aware of us, and of each other, and of everything we know? And why should they be interested in talking to us or to each other?

I start with "A Model of Our Minds on the Other Side," which gives us a way to see the interaction of our lives in the three-dimensional physical world and the greater life that exists on the non-physical side of things.

"The Individual as Convenient Fiction" reinterprets our lives and essence, showing that what we think we know about ourselves is true only partially, and only from a particular point of view.

"The Physical and the Non-Physical" sets out, as plainly as possible, the differences and interactions between the two sides of the metaphorical veil. This chapter, more than any other, shows how and why our lives here are important to both sides.

Chapters Four and Five, "Living Connected" and "Shaping Your Life," move from description of *what is* to suggestions about *what you can do* to live a life that is richer, more satisfying, more meaningful.

Let's begin with a model of how we function on the other side, as described by the guys upstairs.

Chapter One

A Model of our Minds
on the Other Side

*And I thought sitting up awake in the African night that I knew
nothing about the soul at all. People were always talking of it and
writing of it, but who knew about it? I did not know anyone who
knew anything of it nor whether there was such a thing.*
—[From *True At First Light*, a posthumous book from
Ernest Hemingway's abandoned attempts, page 172.]

*Higher consciousness, or knowledge going beyond our present-day
consciousness, is equivalent to being all alone in the world.*
—C.J. Jung, *The Archetypes And The Collective Unconscious*. Page 169

*[Hemingway's intellectual dilemma was typical of his time and
ours. Thinking about the soul and about death, he was led to realize that he didn't know anything about either one. In the absence
of a believable concept of an afterlife, many people assume that the
only alternatives are pretending to believe in heaven and hell or to
disbelieve in any afterlife at all. But the fact that we are unable to
envision heaven is not proof that it does not exist. It may be proof*

1

merely of lack of imagination, or lack of data. It does suggest that there is a serious mis-match between religious descriptions and their intended audience . . . as TGU explains below.]

Contradictory Story

Your sciences, your theologies, your arts and letters, may be judged by whether they shape a common understanding of what it is to be a human in the world—of what it means that there *is* a world, of what the nature is of what actually exists. A unified, coherent culture, such as ancient Egypt or medieval England to a lesser extent, or an American Indian family to an even lesser extent, *sees things whole.*

Contemporary 20th and 21st century cultures do not, because for one thing they must try to incorporate too many incompatible features, and for another they have too many neighbors (the same thing said another way) and for a third thing *none of them has the key.* So long as cultures are grown upon the wrong understandings they cannot be made unitary save by force—and this is not unity, only the appearance and the imitation of unity, which will dissolve or explode in a flash. It is typical of your times that the very point we have just raised will be little understood without explanation. Some will say, what does chemistry have to do with theology, or either with economics, or any of the three with novels, say? So let us circle back to our theme.

Consider first the sciences, which make the easiest entry to the subject. Sciences begin as a poking around among phenomena, looking for the reality beyond appearances, seeking to deduce the laws of behavior that produce the phenomena. In other words, a science may be described as the abstraction into "laws" of the deduced causes of observed behavior. As each successive layer of phenomena is abstracted and understood, successively more internal layers are investigated and comprehended.

Sometimes the new layers make it obvious that previously accepted rules of thumb (so to speak) were too generalized, too rough and ready, and so the previously formed laws are refined. Sometimes new investigations trigger a landmine that blows up part of the previous structure, as for example the discovery of x-rays did. Now, what is this process but the ongoing construction of story to connect perceptions? The story is modified to fit perception, and is modified repeatedly—and in fact scientists are proud of the process, thinking they are all the while advancing upon "truth" which *in a way* they are. But the way that they are doing so is less in the new story they construct than in the previous story they discard! That is, scientific investigation may be looked upon as an ongoing demolition of previous story. (It rarely *is* looked at that way, of course, but it validly might be.)

It should be obvious to you now that the fact that a story can be elaborated and modified and even partially torn down and rebuilt differently is no guarantee that it is anything more than a story connecting perceptions! It should be obvious that the more the elaborations (mathematical and otherwise) on the story, the more persuasive it becomes, and the greater the investment in it people have, particularly those whose livelihood depends on it, and who have invested years of intellectual investment in it. Science is not truth; it is story constructed around perception.

Similarly, metaphysics and religion. The perceptions are real and cannot be doubted by those who have experienced them—but in the nature of things, the structure built upon them is—story. To say it is *story* is not to say that it is *fiction*. It is merely to repeat that it is the result of people playing connect-the-dots around what they know or sometimes think they know. What are scriptures but extensive records of perceptions? What are the religions built upon the scriptures but story added to them, to try to make sense of them? What is art but story, making patterns of perceptions?

All right, we think that is about as clear as we can put it. Now—assuming that you agree with us so far—what does it imply? For of course you can't live in the world without story, express and implied. And that statement itself is part of what we wish to say. *You cannot live without story,* for story is how you make sense of the world. But it is useful to remember that there is a difference between story and reality, and while everyone is willing to agree to that abstractly, in practice it is usually forgotten. Remembering the fact will save you from dogmatism and from despair, from premature certainty and from mistaken certainty that nothing can be known well enough to form a basis for life, if only "good enough for government work."

It can be seen that no one can possess absolute truth—that is, a story that correctly takes into account all perceptions (or rather what there is to be perceived) in their proper relationships. Yet *some* story is needed to be going along with. The best story is one that incorporates the most elements, that reconciles the most perceptions or, we should say, the greatest number of *most-important* perceptions, for one most-important perception is worth millions of true but unimportant perceptions (if you can be sure which category is which!).

A society is built upon many stories. The less they contradict each other, the more harmonious the society (though that does not guarantee that the story is true, just that it is more consistent). A society that tries to live by self-contradictory story wracks itself to pieces, as you see around you. Your sciences are essentially materialist at core; your religions are essentially dogmatic at core; your arts recognize no responsibility to express the deepest truths they find, nor do they have any firm basis for expressing what they perceive. The arts, the sciences, the religions, are all headed in different directions, within themselves and when compared one to another. *Does this not tell you that they are ungrounded in reality?* Truth converges. They are built upon sand, and the shifting of the sands will destroy them. Society cannot build upon rock while its story tells it that there is no rock (science), and that they are already upon rock (religion), and that we cannot yet tell whether rock exists, and that whether rock exists is a matter for personal opinion (art).

Religious Understandings

It is well if you remember that explanations are analogies. Only that which does not need to be explained can be presented as itself. Everything else has to be explained as "like" the nearest similar thing—as Bruce Moen [author of several books on exploring the afterlife] well explains. You can say that the color orange is "like" red, and also "like" yellow—a statement that is incomprehensible to anyone who has experienced red and yellow but not orange—or you can say "orange" knowing that the observer has already experienced orange. In the strictest sense, explanations always mislead to some extent, regardless of the best efforts of the explainers. You know, or you do not yet know, and there can be no third position. Explanation is a bridge between the two that sometimes bridges and sometimes collapses.

Mankind has mostly believed in a personal God or gods, who interested Himself or Themselves in humans and their affairs. There is a reason for this and it is not because your ancestors were superstitious lunatics who confused "natural" events and "supernatural" causes. The reason people invented gods is that they had *experienced* them!

Here in a nutshell is how humans invented gods. The *experiences* were undeniable. The *presence* and their *interest in humans* were felt. Older eras, being more open to things your age is only beginning to reawaken to, had no doubt: The *perception* was shared among the members of each community. But of course each community created its own *story* about the perceptions, and hence as formerly isolated communities came into contact, they discovered that their neighbors worshipped other gods. If they were tolerant of each other this did no harm. If they were not, their neighbors were worshiping *false* gods, or competing gods, and must if possible be destroyed. Here it is your key to the early books of the Bible: genuine perception, inflated story—result, repeated genocide, or attempted genocide.

But the underlying perceptions of an extra-worldly (so to speak) superhuman presence taking a very real interest in human affairs socially and individually was accurate. The rise of the higher religions may be seen as the ascent of greater abstraction. That is, the sense of the diversity of forces was subsumed into a stronger sense to the underlying unity behind forces.

So the Muslims cry out in testimony, "There are no gods, but only God," and this is saying (in a sense) "the world is not a contending chaos, but a conscious design." This was well and good, but it had the result of emphasizing one set of characteristics (design) over others (chaos, for instance, or free will). The Hindus seized upon the multiplicity of forces, subdividing them far more than did, say, the ancient Greeks and Romans. These hundreds of gods are still believed in and revered, by uncounted millions. Others in that society, Western-oriented, now hold these beliefs in one part of their minds (like Sunday Christians) divorced from practical considerations. Still others scorn them as the superstitions of their stupid ignorant ancestors (who somehow created a great civilization out of their stupidity and superstitiousness). And your day's materialist scientists concentrate on laws—on the impersonal aspects of the creation—and correspondingly undervalue the antithetical aspects, as is only natural. From our point of view this is productive, as one society emphasizes one set of characteristics and another seizes upon another, either radically different or largely overlapping or anywhere in between.

You see what we are saying? Each of these perceptions, save the last, is followed by story that results in a personal God or gods. The last—the secular West—systematically removes from consideration any perceptions that argue that the other side interacts continually on an individual or societal basis.

Totally as an aside, we point out to you that this is the

reason for religions of all kinds, including scientism: People can only be brought along from where they are. If the explanation is too simple for them, they fall away from that religion and go seeking something more satisfying. If too advanced for where they are, they have no attraction for it—no velcro, as you would say—and so either are never aware of it or discard it as obvious nonsense. But if it is at their level, it can minister to their needs on the unspoken assumption that the individual is one part of a larger body, rather than an isolated meaningless individual. A person in a community of people gathered within a religion that is right for them is much like the army experience that Joseph Smallwood described. There is that exalted feeling—we do not mean egotism or psychic inflation—of being a part of something vastly larger. That is a true feeling, recognized as true whenever experienced, regardless what Story is wrapped around the Perception.

The paragraph above would repay close attention.

The Spiritual Problem of Western Civilization

You are coming to realize that what we are giving you here is the root of the problem of Western civilization, nothing less. And that is: Being unable to believe in immortality, or being unable to conceive of immortality as anything but a vague continuation of existence, because of conclusions that for a while seemed forced by reason in the light of science, western civilization split into three parts, each regarding itself as the only legitimate and accurate representation of reality, and therefore as the only legitimate authority around which society was to revolve, thus setting the scene for endless struggles.

So you have those who follow scriptural authority (religion), others who follow investigative authority (science) and still others who follow instinct informed (depending on the person) by different combinations of scriptural and scientific information.

Each of these has a different worldview. Each in a very real sense lives in a different world. They perceive different facts, deduce different rules, arrive at different conclusions.

Each division can be subdivided. Catholics and fundamentalists and Quakers have huge differences among them, not to mention the differences between any of them and Muslims, Rastafarians, Hindus or Buddhists. Nonetheless, you can see a rough commonality among them. Similarly, physicists live in a pretty different world from sociologists, and either from psychologists, yet they all look to experientially derived data for their authority. And Goethe may have significant differences from Ken Kesey, and each from Hemingway, say—but they are all making sense of the world less from scripture or scientific investigation than from personal intuition.

Again, this is only a classification scheme. Goethe could be put in among scientists, as could Thoreau. Newton had a foot in at least two worlds. The point is not to pick holes in the scheme but to pick an inferred *whole* out of it. For this is what it gives you, you see. Once you see the culture as consisting of a positive, a negative and a reconciling force (to use Gurdjieff's terms) you see that *none of the three may be dispensed with*. Each is necessary, and will be present one way or another. It is not the presence or even the overdeveloped presence of any that is the problem. The problem of the West—and hence of the world—is not that there are three ways of receiving data but that the three appear to be delivering *contradictory* data! In spelling out to you a scheme of what life is really like, and in pointing out that the means of personal verification are available to each of you, we propose to give you the clue that society could follow to reunify its vision. As could you as an individual.

If *scientists* as *scientists* (not as individuals with divided minds, putting their science aside on Sunday mornings, so to speak) could obtain first-hand knowledge of the essential immortality and interpenetrating nature of life—

If the *religious as seekers of religious truth* could interpret their experience in light of the scriptures (and then, soon enough, learn to use the scriptures as roadmaps of what they are likely to discover, or should watch out for, or tools that they may be able to use)—

If the *poets and mystics as intuiters of truth* could fashion a reconciling view respecting both religion and science—

Do you not then have your next civilization in its essence? You will not live long enough to see it flower but you may easily live long enough to see it take root—and you will continue to actively participate (with greater freedom and sureness) from the other side.

Your model of consciousness is wrong, and so you understand things wrong. Of course, your model is wrong because you understand things wrong, too—it is a feedback loop, Models *reflect* understandings from experience, while *distorting* or at least *molding* understandings from experience, which means, in practice, *limiting* possible experience. But never mind that. The point is that your model of consciousness is wrong. We will give you another model (if your fear of contradicting authority does not disable you as intermediary) and the new model will enable you to see things differently, by freeing you from exclusive reliance on the old inadequate models. Let's look at them.

Old Models of Consciousness

First model. You have a body. You are confined physically to the time and space that your body occupies. If you think that neither soul nor mind exists, you think that the physical conditions surrounding the body determine what only *seem to be* mental and spiritual processes. This is the extreme position—that you are only a body; that anything you think is the result of what your body experiences, that if you could know everything it experiences, you would be able to account for everything you think, and everything you *seem to* feel; everything you *seem to* intuit.

People who are unable to subscribe to the idea that the body accounts for everything split into two camps. One camp adds mind, another adds mind and spirit. The model that sees the individual as body and mind—the second model—implies a dualism that wonders which is master, which is servant. In any two-fold scheme, one is primary and one secondary: There can be no equality of being in any mixture. So one believing in this model is driven to the position of saying one is *primarily* a body upon which mind has grown, or one is *primarily* a mind that has manifested a body. Historically both ways of seeing it are represented. For the moment let us leave it at this: the points of view that see only body and mind tend to see *a* body and *a* mind, and they differ as to which is primary.

Psychological experience convinces others that the body/mind scheme is inadequate. Life tells them that they are composed of body and mind and spirit, a third model. (Your society very loosely mixes the terms spirit and soul, not knowing the difference, hence not knowing how to distinguish between them. But this anticipates.) The third level is body *and* mind *and* what is termed spirit, an immaterial "something" that is necessary to life. No spirit, no life. Extinguish life, destroy the bond between body and spirit. We have no quarrel with that view. In practical terms, "it works." The spirit is the "something" that gives life. No one shapes spirit; nor does spirit shape our lives. Spirit *animates*, it provides the vital link that "keeps body and soul together," as the old saying is. But it is not particular to the individual in any detail. Like the wind, to which it is often compared, spirit blows where it wants to blow, according to its own laws of being. *There is nothing personal about spirit.* Yet—you must hold the contradiction—spirit is a closer part of you than anything else, and so may equally justly be described as *entirely personal* in the way people experience it. To put it again, because you are part of spirit, you experience it entirely personally. Because spirit is so vast and apparently animates everything, it is in its essence far beyond personality. So—personal *and* impersonal. The breath of life (how often have you heard it called that, and not really heard what was being said) and yet the animation of worlds. This is stuff of the gods. We will return to it.

A fourth model includes the soul, and for the moment we will say that this is the model we prefer. Those who perceive body *and* mind *and* spirit *and* soul see now (at least) a four-fold being, not nearly as simple and unitary as first appeared. *This is not merely what you may have heard, or heard about, as church doctrine.* Hear us: We are describing something real, not something deduced or invented. We have no agenda provided by a church or religion. (Indeed, they will likely regard us as illegitimately poaching on their privatized soil.) Your soul has as much to do with the color of your hair and your taste in paintings and the kind of jokes you prefer as it does how "good" or "evil" you are. It concerns your weight, your talents, your amusements, your illnesses, your irrational preoccupations. It incorporates the effects of your home life, your commuting to an office, your paying taxes, your playing games. It includes your best and worst moments, your pets, your car, your house as they interact with you—in short, *your life.* You might look upon the soul as the flower you create in the living of your life. Where the spirit *animates*, the soul *personifies.*

All your life, you choose what you are going to be. You learn this, you bypass that, you encourage these threads of behavior, you choose (deliberately or otherwise) not to encourage others. You *do*, and in *doing* you are *being.* You choose, continually, from the many choices presented to you—for any situation presents choices, if no more than a choice of how to react to the inevitable. As you continually choose, you continually shape your soul. The soul is the photograph of your being, a photograph that changes as you change it. It is who you are. It is the template by which you could be recreated if one had sufficient skill, materials and tools. Where the spirit is impersonal in that it cannot be shaped by your life, the soul is entirely personal, and is entirely shaped by your living of its potentials.

The body holds you in one time and place at a time, and drags you (kicking and screaming sometimes!) to the next moment, and the next. The mind observes, participates, directs, learns, reacts, concludes, resolves—and in short provides the awareness needed for the body to function in its surroundings. The spirit provides the energy that fuels body and mind moment by moment. Unseen, unfelt, unfailing, it is the background that is unseen *because* it is the universal support. Being universal, its presence in has to be inferred, practically, for in time-space there is no place where it is not. And the soul is the local manager of the body-mind-spirit combination. It is the universal record of this particular expression of life. It incorporates every moment, first to last. Life is about choosing who and what you want to be. The result of all this choice becomes the soul, so that it might be said, truly enough (from one viewpoint) that a lifetime *begins with* spirit and body, *adds* mind, and *grows* soul.

True enough for rough estimates. But, having come this far, we have to say that this model we just sketched is as wrong (from our viewpoint) as the earlier models we reject, because it assumes solidity where there is only flow, and identity where there is only community.

Take the body. You have learned to separate it conceptually into four—physical, energetic, mental, emotional. As working definitions these work well enough. The physical body is made up of a huge number of sub-systems, each of which functions autonomously and well. Is it one body with subsystems or is it many intelligences cooperating to produce a functioning whole? Either view is true enough. Hold the thought a while.

The energetic body is a subsystem of the physical body. It is a subsystem large enough, autonomous enough, that it is worth considering separately for specific purposes. By definition its purpose is to provide the energetic superstructure of the physical body. Without the energetic body the physical body could not function. Equally, without the physical body the energetic body would have no reason for being.

The mental body is a representation of an interaction between "mind" and "body." Touch a spot inside the brain with an instrument, and a memory appears, as fresh as the day it was imprinted. (Whether the spot is actually the carrier of the memory or the gateway to storage elsewhere is immaterial.) The brain could be mapped, if one knew how to do it, so that the memories were located and labeled, and so could the entire body. Traumas of all sorts are located at different parts of the body, so that a massage therapist may press on a calf muscle and find that the client responds by breaking into tears at the strength of a suddenly remembered event from long before. Thus conceptually one might map the body's stored areas of trauma and other experience. The emotional body, similarly, is a representation of where the body stores *emotional* memory.

Now, all these substructures, these subsystems, are what we might call logical derivations of function. In a way they do *not* exist except as useful abstractions. In a way they *do* exist in that, as conceptualizations, they offer a way to work with the underlying reality. And what do you want beyond something that works? The trick is to prevent useful tools from becoming superstitions.

Again, remember that this entire model is in our view not a good model for what humans are. You now require a better model, and this we propose to give you.

The Physical and the Non-Physical

We begin by moving your point of reference. Much of the reason why current models do not lead you to larger understandings stems from the idea that the physical body is primary, which of course stems from the idea that the physical, itself, is primary. It is not. Bear in mind, in the course of this argument we are going to ignore or merely deny certain points of view that would otherwise entangle us in argument to no purpose. Let those who wish to deny the existence of the non-physical do so. We will not worry ourselves or you about how to "prove" that the physical is not primary, or, indeed, that the non-physical exists. Those unable to entertain our point of view will go elsewhere—will *remain* elsewhere—and no harm will be done.

The physical is dependent for its existence upon a deeper level of reality that by definition is not subject to time and space. Please try not to jump to religious categories of thought as soon as you find yourselves considering the non-physical. It is true that religious thought attempts to convey that reality, but it is equally true that *it fails*. It fails, as we shall fail, because "three into two doesn't go," as the old saying is. That is, translating the greater into terms of the lesser must necessarily result in serious distortion. Symbols distort less than precise language, but distortion cannot be avoided. We prefer to deal with this fact by either creating different analogies or by setting out competing viewpoints, so that the unsayable truth may be somewhat perceived between the lines. Of course "two analogies" or "two viewpoints" is much the same thing, for our most careful statement must yet be an analogy, just from the nature of things. If these things could be said and conveyed, they would have been said long since. But the very structure of your language necessarily contains the assumption of the reality of forces and conditions that (in our view, from "where" we are) do not exist, or anyway do not much resemble your experience of them or your conclusions from your experience.

Chief among the characteristics that condition the physical realm and not the non-physical are that time is experienced in slices, and therefore life is experienced as separation and delayed consequences. Let us begin simply with these. The relevance of all of this to our model of reality will become apparent.

Time-slices. You experience the world as past, present, future. They seem to you to be real conditions within which you must live, because the structure of your language insists on structuring into any thought a sense of time passing. How you experience past, present and future will vary by culture, and by language, and by mental or emotional state, but the three concepts will be there.

Because you experience your lives this way, certain realities are fundamentally distorted.

Because of separation in space, you experience yourself as in one body and others as in other bodies. Your sense of separation may be somewhat modified by your *ideas*, your *theoretical* life, but you will continue to experience yourself as a separate body functioning in a world that is primarily "other." If you lose an arm or a leg in an accident, that arm or leg becomes part of the "other"—and if you were to regenerate a new limb to replace the one you lost, you wouldn't regard the new limb as something "other" that had joined you but as just—part of you. Inconsistently, you say "you are what you eat," which logically means that the "other" becomes part of you and the part of you that you excrete becomes "other" again. If you look at this closely you will see how arbitrary are the distinctions between self and other.

And if you perceive that the heart gives off electrical impulses that interact at a distance of as much as ten feet, this changes your definition of separation so that for, instance, some might now say that no two people within a few feet of each other function entirely separately. This is true as far as it goes but *it will make no difference* in the fact that people will go on considering themselves to be separate. They may admit to being influenced by many subtle forces, but they *cannot* experience themselves as other than separate beings. They may *believe*, they may *conceptualize*, they may *emotionally* experience unity, but in fact and everyday, they feel themselves separate and cannot help but do so. It is in the design of the physical world and therefore *there is nothing wrong* with this. But it does not define ultimate reality, either.

This bias must be taken into consideration. It cannot be eliminated, and will sneak in behind every discussion. You experience yourself as a "you"—as a person—as an individual. How else *could* you experience yourself? So long as you are separated in space—that is, so long as you are in physical matter—you cannot experience yourself in any other way. Once more: This is how it was set up to work, so it shouldn't be a surprise that it works this way.

However . . . .

Now we invite you to convey yourself beyond what your physical life convinces you is real. To do so—given your surroundings, which most emphatically includes your language!—requires a thought-experiment. First we will set up the experiment. Then, *do* the experiment! Try. You will not succeed, perhaps, but the *effort* will help you to understand and appreciate and see beyond the analogy that we will suggest beyond the experiment.

So—here is the experiment. Assume for the moment that you are in actual literal fact part of everyone and every thing else; that only your spatial environment is convincing you that separation is reality. How could you conceive of that in a way that you would find intellectually respectable? Perhaps you can't *feel* that lack of separation; how could you theoretically imagine it? Do the experiment.

No, we mean really, do the experiment. The printed words aren't going anywhere, but this is the only time you will be able to do the experiment with exactly these mental and physical conditions surrounding you. Do the experiment. If you were to imagine yourself and all the "other" as part of one thing, what could you imagine as the situation and connections that hold it all together?

Last chance. Did you do the experiment?

All right, here is what we would say to you. You are all assembled from the same huge table of ingredients. You all contain the same chemicals, the same materials; you are assembled according to the same diagrams and schematics; you have similar mental emotional and energetic structures. Well and good;

nobody would quarrel with this. But this is not wherein your unity resides, and your diversity. The key to your unity—and diversity—is hidden from you superficially by separation in space and to a lesser degree by separation in time. We call this key the concept of threads.

Minds on the Other Side

[Explaining a new model is even more difficult than receiving it in the first place. But, one morning, I got the sense that the guys wanted to explain the network of minds by way of a diagram, so that the right brain's pattern-recognition function could interpret it, "because words can explain and amplify and clarify but alone they can only mislead." So I got out a pencil and paper and drew some circles, above and below a line, and as I worked, they chimed in.]

Every conceivable situation exists—some minds are great networkers. Some are much more solitary. But ultimately everyone connects, on either side of the veil. And bear in mind, this is radically simplified. It takes no account of the multiple overlapping layers of relationship that become more obvious as you look more deeply in time and space. Nonetheless you can see that things connect not simply and uniformly like single-cell organisms, but complexly like the physical body. Envision this diagram extending backward into the page and forward from the page—in 3-D in other words—and you will begin to get a visual sense of the complexity that would require some level of drawing skill to suggest.

Pencil in letters for the circles on what you call the other side *[of what is called "the veil" separating the non-physical from the physical world].* Just do it arbitrarily; there is no meaning of hierarchy implied by the letters. Now number your individuals on your side. This will make it easier to describe the process.

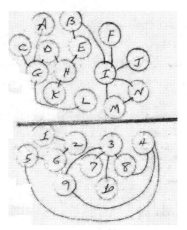

*[This diagram resulted. At the top are minds on the "other side"
of the (non-existent) line between 3-D and non-3-D. Beneath the
line are our minds in 3-D The lines are links of affiliation, temperament, etc. that organize the entire field.]*

Suppose A knows chemistry, B psychology, F practical poli-
tics, and J is an artist. That's enough complexity to be going
along with.

Now if you were to think of these things as *abstractions* you'd
have a logical, probably symmetrical structure, probably pretty
static. But considered as *minds*, you can see that it is much more
dynamic. Perhaps A connects to G because one is parent and
the other is child. Perhaps G in turn connects to C, D and L by
profession, affection, and kinship respectively. (And here you see
the tip of the iceberg of complexity: if G is kin to A and L, L is
in some way kin to A as well as G.)

This is all from one point of view, by the way. Another person's map of the same minds might have some ties more prominent and others less.

Now if a person in physical reality—1, say—wishes to
inquire about chemistry, he may need to talk to A. If they are
close enough in wavelength that it may be done directly, well and
good. If not, then silently and unobserved by 1 or openly and
described to 1 (as a "control," say), whoever 1 can reach links to

A for him. So it may be that 1 can link to I (a good networker). The chain may have to go like this: 1 = I -> B -> E -> H -> D -> G -> A and back! But once 1 and A have once linked up, the intermediate chain may be dispensed with, as they will by the process of information transfer have established a direct link. In a future exchange, 1 could then perhaps go by way of A (silently or explicitly) to reach G, and any that connect via G, by a shorter or more direct route. Thus the network is ever changing.

Note—this beginning of an explanation does not address the question of any active cross-communication that takes place entirely on either side. Neither does it do more than hint at the effects that are made possible by communication of, say, I and A via 1. Thus, Hemingway meets your father [via my mind, both being deceased], and both learn the latest news of Earth (so to speak) which becomes a part of them and changes them—and it all is continually changing and becoming ever more complex.

Influences on the Individual

All right, so let us bring our charts to another level of complexity. Again, do this in pencil so that you will be less prone to anxiety about it, knowing that you (we) don't have to get it "right" the first time. And of course what applies to you applies to many others, who will find our anxiety-avoidance techniques useful, perhaps.

Looking at the basic diagram you just drew, realize that each circle is not a unit but is in itself a complex structure, or meeting-point, or focus (however you would like to think of it) all parts of which may come into play in different circumstances. Let's start on your side for convenience, working this from the familiar to the less familiar (although "familiar" is a very relative term, and in a way could be considered to mean "the unknown that you think you know"). Let's see who 1 really is, what 1 really consists of.

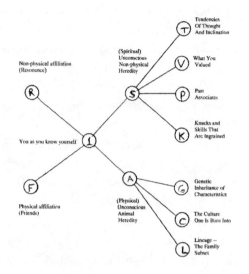

You see we start off with 1A and 1S, your heredity both physical and nonphysical, as Yeats would say. Putting one above and the other below is merely convention: They could just as well be portrayed in reverse order, or side-by-side.

So, you add 1R for *nonphysical* beings with whom you share resonance (thus bypassing questions about reincarnation) and 1F (F for friend) for *physical* beings with whom you share resonance.

Looking at 1A we find: genetic inheritance of characteristics, genetic and habit-formation inheritance through the family, and the overall influence of the culture one is born into. These all affect the individual every day but usually mostly below the threshold of consciousness.

Looking next at 1S for your nonphysical heredity: developed tendencies of thought and inclination, and, closely related to that, skills and knacks developed over repeated lifetimes. Also past associates of the blood or otherwise, which differs from 1R because while you are on the same wavelength with those you resonate with (by definition), any given life will shovel you into relationship with people you don't resonate with. You have some point in common, or you could not meet—but you are not naturally in instinctive sympathy. Nonetheless the shared experience provides a link that otherwise would not be there. (It is one prime advantage of life in the physical that it allows one to associate with others of such different wavelengths that they would never easily meet on this side.) Finally we could add those things which you have loved or valued. If you reread Moby-Dick seven times, or read the Bible every year like Cayce, or if you were an admirer of Napoleon or of Wellington, or if you haunted the opera or the theater, or if you were bonded to animals or trees or loved to play cards or—anything—that old connection survives, perhaps unsuspected or experienced but inexplicable to you.

Of the presence in your psyche of 1F, friends and lovers, there should be no need to say much. This is always well known. The tie between friends or between lovers may be more mysterious or complex—certainly more volatile—than is commonly experienced; nonetheless mammals—and you are mammals while in the body, however you may think of yourselves—cannot live alone without shivering.

Of your nonphysical associates (1R) you have been getting some slow education. If you as a conscious creature in time-space contain all these elements, think how complex is your energy signature! Think how many, many different wave-lengths you may resonate to. It is in physical matter that the universe as we know it gains so many possibilities of self-referencing incremental complexity.

Now, remember that "the physical" does not mean only humans, or only humans and animals, or only humans and animals and vegetables and minerals, and it doesn't mean all the earth or even all the galaxy. It means *all* of the part of creation that exists within sequential time and what that implies (time-slices, delayed consequences) and separation by space and what *that* implies (a seemingly absolute division rather than division into units only provisionally or, shall we say, "somewhat"). Does that include Alpha Centuri the star? Yes. Any of its planets? Yes.

Any lifeforms existing there, whether recognizable as life to you or not? Yes.

Everything that exists in 3-D space is part of the physical aspect of the world. (And we use "the world" here as it used to be used in earlier times, as a synonym for all physical creation.) The reason to stress this point is that you will find an unconscious tendency to divide things between the vast and mysterious and vague "other side" on the one hand and on the other hand not all creation, but only earth, or often enough, only humans. That would be a total absolute distortion and is to be avoided. You see, the interaction we are painting is not a matter of humans on one side and us on the other side. It is not even a matter of Earth life on one side. It is *all* physical matter anywhere, even if Earth never hears of it. How else could it be? Could you have only a local part of the universe, and not all, in connection with the other side?

Now consider what we are saying. You Downstairs, on your side, connect with us Upstairs, or on our side. We in turn connect with others on your side. Some of those others may live on Alpha Centuri, or in far galaxies of which you will never get a glimpse or have an inkling. Do you think they are any farther from us (where space is not local, nor time) than you are? And since both you and they may connect *to* us, obviously one potential for your communication as it improves is that you can communicate *through* us, and ultimately *without* us.

Welcome to the universe.

And there is more than that. Since you by your decisions affect us and they by their decisions affect us, and we reciprocally affect you and them—in essence to greater or lesser degree, more consciously or less, *you affect each other*. Really, you each affect reality, which affects each of you, but it comes to the same thing.

You see, physical matter, with its delayed consequences and its ability to form ever more complex relationships among its inhabitants, is central to the universe (the world; we need a bigger term; to physical and nonphysical reality considered as one).

Do you still feel like insignificant inhabitants of a third rate planet circling a sixth-grade star at the edge of the universe, or does that view begin to look a bit myopic?

Redefining Ourselves and the World

And still the picture is not even nearly complete. You may contact all the past, all the future, anyone and everyone in the physical or nonphysical part of the world. The key is to redefine yourselves, redefine the world, so as to disconnect the thought-systems that disable you by persuading you that it is not possible. It is that simple, that easy, that overwhelmingly powerful.

"But?" For you must feel the presence of an implied "however," or why hasn't everyone done it? Merely, it is harder to do as individuals than as part of the herd. The pioneers have to contend against the specific gravity of the species, so to speak. It is harder to do what hasn't been done, because one's internal weigher of probabilities and possibilities exerts a formidable drag. The Wright Brothers were aided immeasurably not only by all those who had attempted to build flying machines but—more, in fact—by those who had opened their minds to the possibility of practical flight and had thus hacked invisible paths into the surrounding jungle of certainty that it couldn't be done. A positive confident attitude did not by itself provide the formulas and experience that led to success, but it did help in ways that are scarcely suspected and never seen.

Anyone reading this and listening to that inner voice saying "yes, that's the way it is; this actually can be done, though it is going to require work and practice"—just *listening* to the voice helps break the logjam. Making your own attempts helps more. Overcoming your own skepticism and making the effort to not negate results by declaring that you made it all up helps even more. Working with friends is another step. Coming out into the open about your experiments and your experiences adds vastly to the effect. And so it goes, as each one pioneers as best he or she can. Every attempt—even if made in silence in a darkened room on an island without telephones, so to speak—adds its weight to the scales. We see so clearly on the side what you often have to strain to bring yourselves to believe—*every effort counts*. You all create together, even when working separately. And (it should be obvious but, we would bet, isn't until we say it)—so do we.

It is from lack of a plausible model more than from any other single thing that the division between seen and unseen world has come to seem so absolute. Well, we've given you a model to work with. More, we are giving you the tools to do your exploring (and hence your model-repair) with. Everything you need has been given. It is up to you to do it, or to decline to do it.

Life as Preparation

When new material is breaking out in profusion and you feel old understandings becoming inadequate, that is the time to set out the older ones for what they will do later—that is, so they will not be lost. And the setting-out of where you are will provide a firm base for future developments, as happened when you wrote *Muddy Tracks*. So—one more incentive, and a major one.

This represents a break in pattern for you, and so is a bigger step than you realize, as is the nature of steps in general. Any big step is more than you realize in advance, even if you realize in advance that it is a big step. That is, you may know that "if I can bring myself to do this, I will be overcoming a huge internal obstacle," but even then you are unlikely to be able to sense what life beyond the big step is going to be. This is not a profound or complicated thought, but it is important to realize it. It's the old story about maps and explorations. If you really move into new territory, how can you know in advance what it looks like? You may have maps drawn by other people, and they may be accurate maps, but until *you* go there, you won't have had the experience of the place. How *can* you have had it? That's the purpose of traveling instead of merely memorizing maps.

It is usually an illusion to think that your life is continuity merely because it is flow. Or perhaps we should say, flow tends to enhance your perception of life as continuity by dulling your perception of life as a series of segues. Or are you the same person in terms of values and ideas and understandings and experience that you were at age 15, say, or 30?

Continuity of memory assures you that you are the same person you were, but in fact continuity of memory is, in a sense, the main, nearly the *only*, way in which you might be described as being the same. For the rest, every new life circumstance brings more into play differing members of your person-group, changing the composition of the active members, which changes how you experience yourself, and how people experience you.

This is commonly experienced as a change (a *continual* change) in external circumstances. But external circumstances and inner circumstances may be regarded as two expressions of the same thing, which is why you will either be the perpetual victim of external events or the creator and shaper of *external* events by means of your shaping of *internal* events. Powerful stuff! And even if you know that you create (in effect) your external life by creating your internal life, you may continue to experience your life *as if* your externals were changing "magically" to meet your deepest needs. But how you experience it doesn't matter, really; it's a matter of taste. What is important is the knowledge—that *practical* knowledge—that you can control your life's externals.

What may be less evident is that the goal of controlling your life's externals, which seems so important and transformative before you get there, is in fact merely an unimportant side-effect.

What? An unimportant side-effect, to be able to control your lives? Yes, because the change itself doesn't matter. You've been shaping your lives right along. What *does* matter is that you know *that* you're doing it, and *how* you're doing it, and—most important perhaps of the three—*why* you're doing it.

To know *that* you shape your external life, in a direct way unsuspected by your society's dominant thought, which says that you are victims, is to know that you have nothing to fear.

To know *how* you're doing it is to hold that pattern in your heads, and give you joy and peace that are not possible while you feel yourself the victim or potential victim of outside forces.

To know *why* you're doing it—well, now you're getting somewhere. Now you've gotten the key to the meaning of your life *to you.*

Once someone is dead and their life is complete—Hemingway, for instance—do you think it matters to them that they took this turn instead of that turn, that they brought forth this set of threads rather than that set of threads at a given time?

If I'm hearing you correctly, you're saying that the physical effects of our internal decisions are less important, because transitory, than the internal effects. But that's seemingly the opposite of how you were saying it.

We stand amended. That's what we are aiming at. Your lives are important, and so therefore are the circumstances of your lives. Never doubt that. But important *how*, and *for what purpose?* *That* understanding makes all the difference.

Sure, every step forecloses opportunities, but, as we've said, every step also brings new ones. It isn't true, though it may look like it, that life is a progressively more constricted pen into which you have been herded. The reason it seems so, or can seem so, is that the externals are progressively less necessary in order to manifest internals, and it is in manifesting *internals*, by dealing with their projection as *externals*, that life consists.

Your life on earth is preparation. It is your life after you have shaped your mind—your soul—by choices made in the earth environment, that counts. So, as we said, your learning to control your life's externals is mere side-effect. It's worthwhile to do, freeing you up for more advanced tasks, but in itself it would be pretty useless, or let's say would be of limited interest, like re-reading Hemingway's schoolboy compositions or his early reporting as he learned his trade.

However, that said, it is a big thing that you learn that your internal life is what controls your external life.

Did I corrupt that sentence? In finishing it I had the sense that somehow logic was overcoming perception.

Yes. Good. And the more you learn to catch such events, the better for your listening. That is, think of it as a feedback loop. You listen, you discern, and the next time you listen with greater discernment. Story becomes ever less important and perception becomes ever *more* important.

To rephrase the thought that you found your logic corrupting: When you learn that your internal life is the important thing in your life, and the externals, though no less real, are there to support and illustrate the internal life, several life-affirming changes occur within you.

- It teaches you that your physical life is an important experience that is only Act I; it is meaningless when seen only in itself (and of course the further acts are invisible from the physical standpoint, leading those who believe only in the physical to conclude that life *is* meaningless).

- It teaches you that you are not alone because it's impossible for anyone to be alone, regardless of externals.

- It teaches you that your own life is endlessly fascinating if approached from a point of view that expects to see the miracles of the everyday. Your *own* life, not only other people's. Hemingway is famous and you are not, so his life is obviously fascinating and yours is obviously drab, right? Enough experience of the internal world shows you that this isn't true, because it couldn't be.

Grounding the Model

[It is one thing to consider a new model. It is another to accept it as a guide. Deciding to begin to use it is still another. We can't use ideas until we can ground them, make them practical.]

Only you hold the particular mixture of thought, memory, high ideals, low practice, ideas, and experiences that are yours. Surely self-evident? Therefore only you will produce whatever you produce on any given day, let alone your entire lifetime. Now, it is well possible that a given person produces nothing noticeable on any given day, or even in an entire lifetime. It is not, however, even *possible* for that person to produce nothing internally. Every given lifetime is a flower created by the living of it, through the successive choices a person makes. Every flower is different because every soul is different. And we smile to see you perceive so quickly that today we want to talk about the formation of a soul. Let us define terms and illustrate them with homely examples.

There is *spirit*. Spirit is eternal. It is the essence of life, the essence behind, and underlying, material life. It is the energy or essence of God, if you will, as it extends into, and creates, physical life. In so far as we are discussing human lives, Spirit is the animating principle, and it is as if separated into individual manifestations. Note the words "as if" because in fact spirit cannot be limited or bound or separated into discrete units.

However, as you deal with your fellow humans, it will seem that way: As you recognize that each human incorporates spirit, your senses and your separation into time-slices and space-slices will lead you—mislead you—into seeing each as having a spirit particular to each, rather than the counter-intuitive but nonetheless more correct perception of each sharing in an undivided spirit.

So. You saw the movie "Seven Years in Tibet." When it came time for the 14th Dalai Lama to be born, Spirit animated the conception of the body, as it would have to animate any conception. The *body* was formed of the substance of his parents' bodies—specifically their physical inheritance, which provided and limited the traits available for him to manifest in this particular lifetime. Again, without the cooperation of the spirit there could have been no living child, but do not in your exploration of abstract relations forget that there could have been no living child, either, without a body! But the child that was born was born a mixture of old and new, and here is where we may lose some. For what is a *soul*? (Remembering what you know of your own life, Frank, and your own life, reader of this, and remembering what you know of the lives of others, you can ground this difficult discussion so that it is meaningful and connects to your everyday life. What good is abstract theory that never connects?) The little boy who would become (or who already was, or who was and was not yet) the 14th Dalai Lama was a little boy! He was a child, without experience. He had certain noticeable traits such as curiosity and enthusiasm and mechanical ability. He was already fashioned in certain directions, one might say, yet he was an ignorant pilgrim as anyone must be, entering into human life.

And yet he was not! The reason he was discerned (not selected) as the reincarnation of the 13th Dalai Lama is that as an infant he passed many tests of knowledge, correctly discerning which of similar items had been the 13th incarnation's possessions and which had not. Where did that knowing come from? *Yet he was a child, not knowing how he knew.* Indeed, early in life it is the things one *knows* that may be relied upon. The things one is taught by rote or experience are often far less reliable.

Try to stay with us here. This will produce an effect of fatigue because it is hard work to follow an unfamiliar working-out of a concept, particularly if it must be hacked out of much that is (or seems) similar, or is intertwined with what is partially false or misleading. Make the effort and you will see that it is its own reward.

A soul may be regarded as being created with a new life. In other words, when spirit and body produce another individual, that individual begins to shape itself. Thus, in being different from what created it, it may be regarded as something distinct. If you have a child, that child is clearly separate from the parents, even though the child is a continuation *in a way* of the parents.

That new life—that new soul, the indivisible part of the new being that has been created—is a separate creation, but not creation out of nothing. Use what you know of physical conception: Each new being contains half the genetic heredity of each parent. Similarly, the soul is not created out of nothing, but out of other what we might call "soul stuff"—other bundles of experience of life. Some of those lives may be lives on earth, some, lives elsewhere. That is not our concern at the moment.

You, Frank, as a boy *knew* that if you read your history books a certain way (a way that you couldn't actually discover) you could alter the past, and make it come out differently. Where would you get such a strange knowing? It was not a casual idea, not a whimsical thought, certainly not anything anyone would ever teach you. You *knew* even while your acculturated mind "knew better" because it "didn't make sense." How does anyone come into life *knowing* certain things while *at the same time* being ignorant of the life they are going to lead?

Your souls are not "just" the continuation of other lives. Neither are they spiritual orphans, so to speak. They are new creations that are the repositories—trustees—stewards (it is hard to find a proper metaphor) for certain strands of soul-stuff that are to experience another human life. Just as your physical heredity combines *half* of one parent and *half* of the second parent, not all of either, so your non-physical heredity contains (not half, but some) of one strand, some of another.

You are not born into lifetime after lifetime (changed by the experiences of each successful life) although it seems like that to you. Neither are you born into a lifetime with no heredity at all.

It is a problem of definitions. As long as you put yourself in the center of your life, you will not understand. When you realize that "you"—your body, your soul—is only one facet of a far greater you, then you will begin to get a sense of at least how things are *not*, if you cannot glimpse how they *are*.

Chapter Two

The Individual as Convenient Fiction

. . . we are confronted, at every new stage in the differentiation of consciousness to which civilization attains, with the task of finding a new interpretation appropriate to this stage, in order to connect the life of the past that still exists in us with the life of the present, which threatens to slip away from it.
—C.G. Jung, *The Archetypes And The Collective Unconscious*, p. 157

And of course the inner processes are very patient. The puzzle of humanness is apparently not meant to be a simple affair to be easily mastered. Whatever deals with human lives is naturally patient.
—Wilson van Dusen, *The Natural Depth in Man*

The Complicated Human Existence

A human being is very complicated. It is a temporary collaboration of many forms of energy, all of which have to work together more or less harmoniously. You shouldn't be surprised when something goes wrong. You should be surprised and grateful that so much goes and remains so right, so long, with so little attention needed from the person-group for whom the work is done.

You are a part of nature, remember. Your body is of the earth—that is, it exists subject to physical laws. It exists only because of the interplay of vast physical forces usually unnoticed. This is not merely a matter of genetics or food and drink and exercise, or a balance of rest and activity. It is not even as simple as proper interplay of electrical and chemical signaling systems, though these are essential. *It is not at all* the automatically functioning mechanism you experience it to be, any more than Star Trek's *Enterprise* is an automatically functioning mechanism.

The control systems, the active monitoring intelligences, function behind the scenes or below decks, or however you want to put it. But the active, functioning, unresting intelligences that run your bodies are of a different order of being than the person-mind recognizes, so it all happens "auto-magically."

The intelligences that coordinate activity to run your bodies are of a different order, because they are shaped for a different order of task. They don't watch Star Trek with you; they monitor the glucose level moment by moment, instead, or they regulate adrenaline, or seek out unwanted presences in your bloodstream and seek to destroy them. At this level your body is run by intelligences very similar to the level of mind that enables a tree root to seek minerals or go around a rock.

So when you do your healing work, on yourselves or on others, this is a layer of intelligence that must be accessed, but obviously you and it do not have a common language. You do not in fact inhabit the same mental world, if you will forgive us describing the intelligence that processes blood sugars as having a mental world. We know that sounds strange to you, but how else would you put it?

At the other end of the scale of cooperating intelligences are minds more like what you are accustomed to, but functioning in a different way because in a different environment and on a different scale. Us, in fact. We see wider, longer, we have vastly more foresight, better perspective, uninterrupted consciousness, if of lower intensity.

And in the middle, still several layers. You as person-mind, living in the moment, coordinating or at any rate surviving the interplay of various strand-minds that are of the complexity to have previously been person-minds themselves. But also you as ultimate coordinator of hidden and uncomprehended forces, more abstract than tangible, in a way. Chakra energies. The organs. Groupings or conceptions you use in addressing your body's intelligences—talking to a shoulder, for instance, finding the underlying cause of a trauma. These concepts you use *work*, but they are only epicycles. And there are all your innumerable past selves *of this lifetime*—you 10 years ago, you on March 12, 1956, etc. (Yes, yes; many of you weren't even alive in 1956; it's just an example.) All this needs to be sorted out into various levels of mind, each with its own characteristics.

It's too much to expect to sketch in all the detail at once. The crucial point was, and is, that the human body-mind is a vast intersection of many types of energy, each of which has its own characteristic intelligence, its characteristic qualities and the defects of those qualities. *Nothing* is dead, or mentally dead, not your fingernails, not your red corpuscles. But you must not expect your red corpuscles to read Milton or do algebra or understand speech or the concept of people. What it does, it does well, and it can only do it well by being designed for it—which means being designed to be *unable* to do things of a nature different from its own. The same may be said of anything, from the simplest kind of mind to the most complex.

Remember this. Just as you came to realize that *everything* in the world is alive, realize that everything partakes in some form of intelligence characteristic to it. A rock's intelligence will not resemble yours any more than its life is even recognizable to you. Nonetheless, if you think any corner of physical creation is without life and without intelligence, you are thinking there is some absolute separation in reality, and there is not. Is not. How could there be?

Why Convenient, Why Fiction

The individual is a convenient fiction. Convenient, because we have to have some way to think about and discuss the "individual" phenomena you know as people, or souls, or spirits, or however you think of them. But fiction, because there is no such thing as an individual—that is, as any one unit—in any meaningful sense of the word. What appears to be a unit is not a unit either in time or in space or in non-physical existence. And this means that it is equally so of those "individuals" without bodies you contact, such as we, now.

The situation that we all find ourselves in, discussing this, is something like the difficulties that arise when you first realize that your bodies are not solid; that matter is mostly space. "You" don't very much exist, nor does the table you write on or the pen you write with. It's all mostly empty space! Yet you write. One body that is mostly empty, contacting another body that is mostly empty, experiences it as equally solid. Your *mind* knows that it is not solid, but that makes no difference. You experience it as being just as solid as you did before you ever heard of atoms and charges.

Similarly, we will talk of how you—and we—are not really individual, and yet you—and we—will continue to experience yourself as individual because it is one of the preconditions of our understanding. But if we at least *know* that our *experience* cannot be trusted absolutely but only approximately, that is still a gain in understanding.

All right, *why* is the individual a convenient fiction—or rather, *how*? Let us list the ways, some of which may seem trivial at first but are equally important.

First, as a biological organism you are of course utterly

dependent upon your environment for your moment-to-moment existence. If you doubt this, merely put your head under water and try to breathe, or attempt to exist without food and drink. We actually hesitated to add this second example as it is not absolute, but for our purposes it will do.

Second, you did not create yourselves (seen as a biological organism) and cannot perpetuate your physical existence beyond death. *You are temporary, because temporal.* And you are the temporary custodian of characteristics and what we might call a physical inheritance from your parents and thus back to the beginning of human existence. You may or may not carry that inheritance into another generation, but you certainly did inherit it. *You did not* create yourself.

Third, you do not maintain yourselves. You require continual input—food of all kinds, including information, emotion, interactions of kinds you cannot even perceive yet are utterly dependent upon. Kept in isolation you would wither and die, particularly if it were possible to keep you isolated from the non-physical world.

Physically, you are dependent upon your surroundings. You did not create yourself and you cannot maintain yourself without cooperation.

On a slightly subtler level, the cells of your body are in continual exchange, and you breathe in the air that was breathed out elsewhere. That's a metaphor, understand. Your body is not a unit nor a self-contained casing except seen at any one moment. You are a flow, not a unit. So is everyone and everything else, and there's nothing wrong with the fact or the situation or the implications.

Slightly subtler still, your *mind* is not a unit, either, but a flow in more senses of the word than one. It flows laterally; it flows in time. Thus, it flows in time as your life flows in time. The things you think, the values you hold, the ideas you are acquainted with, the logical conclusions you draw, the experiences you have absorbed, the situations you respond to—they all change, continually if at different rates, throughout your life. And it would be hard on you if they didn't! Hard, and impossible because events external and internal flow, they never halt, any more than the sun halts in the sky, and for the same reason.

Only outside time-space might *you* be said to exist, really. We know that is paradoxical, but think about it. At any given moment in time, there's a different you. How could that time-bound-you be *you* when the next minute—let alone six years later—brings another? And it is no escape to think—as your time does—that the same you *flowed* in time. If "the same you" can change as radically as you did between age two and now, not to speak of two years from now or even—who knows?—two days from now, where is the *unit* in all that flow? In what way are you the same person that you were 10 years earlier? Your physical organism is a reproduction of the former organism of 10 years ago, replicated cell by cell, but it is not the same. Ask anyone who is aging! Your mental world is not the same, either in ideas or in values or in attitudes or in experience. Your habits, your behavior, your externals—the very things you might think would show the greatest continuity—would astonish you if you could become aware of how completely they have changed as circumstances have changed, even while all you see is continuity.

Within time-space there is no continuity, only flow. It has been well expressed in the saying, "this too shall pass," the only universally applicable, universally true statement ever devised. You can exist as a unit only outside time-space, regardless how you perceive yourselves. But—as we shall try to demonstrate— you cannot do it even there.

Rings and Threads

We have spoken of time and space and separation and delayed consequences. All this was to lay the groundwork so that you may see more clearly that there are other ways of seeing yourselves than as individuals. To us you appear less as individuals made up of something solid than as hollow containers holding together many disparate threads. These threads are characteristics of all kinds.

Imagine a number of rings, linked by threads threaded through, with each thread connecting different rings, seemingly at random. That is, one thread may pass through rings A, B, D, J, Q, and Z while a second may pass through A, J, S, T, and V, and a third may pass through only O and P and a fourth through J, S, P and so forth. We mean to suggest a loose network of rings *connected* by threads, with each thread passing though innumerable rings but not, by far, all or even most of them. Each thread passes through many rings—but skips many. Similarly, each ring gathers many threads, but far from all or even most.

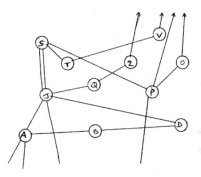

To us you in bodies are the rings, and characteristics are the threads, and to us the threads are as real as the rings. Outside time-space, there is not the same clarity of distinction between "individuals" that space and time impart. Thus, we on "our side" can perceive as solid and tangible something that you on "your side" can perceive only as abstract and theoretical. Thus to us it is permissible to say that left-handedness includes George and Sam, or that drunkenness has Bill and Charlie. This is unfamiliar to you, but after all that's what you are seeking here, is it not, an unfamiliar way of seeing things?

When you learn to see the threads of characteristics running between individuals, you begin to see that it is merely arbitrary to consider individuals as individual. If what seems a "unit" cannot exist without tens of thousands—millions—of components, each of which is shared with uncounted other "units," then it is as true to see that "unit" as one node in a network as it is to see it as a separate item. Either way of seeing it is *somewhat* correct, and either way will allow you to deal with it adequately—but neither description alone is as adequate as both descriptions together.

We can give you an analogy here. As your society's environmental awareness has grown, it has begun to become evident to you that it is as accurate to describe yourselves as sharing the same necessities like air—that is, as being peripheral to the centrality of air—as to describe yourselves as central, with air being merely one of your requirements. If air can get along without you but you cannot get along without air, which has a more independent existence? If water, if food, can get along without you, but not you them, where is the independence of the human? Thus a human might be described—strictly in 3D terms—as an appendage to the environmental systems that sustain life. No air, no water, no relatively stringent temperature range, no chemical preconditions—no humans. That equation cannot be reversed. It is not true to say that removing humans would make impossible the conditions that allow human life.

Now, this is not a lesson in environmentalism or ecology or social science or hard science, so we ask you to return your attention to the point being made. What seem to you in time-space to be individuals—*including yourselves!*—do not look so separate when seen outside time-space. What seem to you in time-space merely abstractions seem a bit more solid and tangible (so to speak) outside time-space. Again, where you see individual rings and mostly do *not* see threads except as abstractions, we see threads as easily and as solidly as rings.

This description of the way we see things should help you to get a clearer image of your situation, and will set the stage for the next step, moving from description to tracing consequences. And those consequences involve a description of how and why you may develop more conscious access to guidance. Perhaps we should say, *ever more conscious* access.

Mind as Habit

We could say, in shorthand, that we regard a mind as a habit-pattern. In outline:

- You are containers—rings—through which pass millions of traits that may or may not manifest externally, but do have the experience of working together as a unit during the lifetime of the body.

- Each of those traits, those threads, may be considered to extend to others, both in the body and not in the body. Thus the threads invisibly connect those who share them.

- Since everyone has millions of them, and since each thread connects with others in and out of body, you can see that you as an individual could consider yourself the center of a vast network of relationships, and so could each of you. We do not mean friendships or blood ties, here, when we say relationships. We mean you are tethered to millions in all directions.

- While you are in the body, the manifestation of such ties is limited in time and space externally, but not of course mentally—for the mind is not physical. Nonetheless when, in the body, you meet someone and it is old

friends meeting, or instant repulsion, this is
not so much past-life stuff, though it may be
that as well, as the recognition of connection
along a given thread or set of threads.

A Unique Collection of Threads

When you have dropped the body—when you have died,
that is—you are no longer under physical constraints on perception or interaction. You *know* what you are, what you connect
with, what vastly indefinite extents you touch. Non-body communication (as opposed to out-of-body, which of course implies
that you are still attached to a body) is unlimited, nonstop, and
you will find it fascinating.

Remember that we said that each thread had its own level
that was its nature, that it vibrates to. (These are physical analogies but after all that is all we have available.) This means that
each set of threads is uniquely connected to others by the combination of vibrations they comprise. If you have 10 threads, num-
bered 1 through 10, you can connect with anything that has any
of those 10 numbers. And if you connect with something that
has one of your numbers—5, say—and also has numbers 20 to
30 (not that there is any sequence implied) then by traveling
down number 5, you can also travel down 20 to 30 and anything
they in turn connect with. In effect, each part connects, directly
or indirectly, with everything. Not only with everything *else* (seen
individually) but with *everything* (seen collectively).

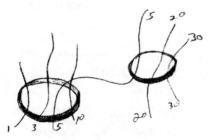

THE COSMIC INTERNET

But each of you is a different collection of numbers. No two will have exactly the same collection, and why should you? (This isn't strictly true, but we resolutely look in other directions for the moment, to avoid the unbelievable complications involved in explaining that too when we are scarcely begun on this. You can have little idea what a handicap to communication it is, having to compress extensions and having to reduce subject matter, so as to fit within the limits of a given mind at a given moment.)

Any given mind shaped on the physical side is going to comprise a given collection of threads that grew together, in effect, during the living of a life. They got accustomed to each other, you might say. They formed a starship crew, or they were a wagon in a wagon train. This *habit* of working together, of considering themselves as "I," is why we refer to minds as habit-systems.

Yet, in the absence of a brain and the rest of the body to filter experience through one time and one place, moment by moment, you can see that each mind, otherwise unchanged, functions differently than when it was so tethered. It is not limited to one set of physical inputs. It is not hampered, or shall we say shaped, by limitations in simultaneous processing of data. It does not experience the physical division into conscious and unconscious (which, we point out, from our view is exactly the reverse of the way you see it, in that your "consciousness" is the part that is nearly entirely unaware of the greater reality, and the surrounding "unconscious" is the part that continues to function normally) and therefore its self-definition is far more accurate and useful.

Understanding Threads

We are proceeding in a straight-line direction. First we showed that you as individuals aren't individual in any meaningful description—despite how a life *feels* separate, often alone.

Then we showed that—as in so many things—it isn't significantly different on this side. Despite popular mythology of many kinds, we aren't the individuals on this end that you may be tempted to think us, any more than on your side. All this, though, certainly should raise the question in your minds—where is the continuity among so much flow? Where is the source of the feeling of individuality that is an inseparable part of life? Further questions should include that of traditional religious belief—how is it that people have come to believe in reincarnation or in judgment followed by heaven or hell, if we are not individuals in the way such ideas seem to require? (The book you published, *The Division Of Consciousness*, by Peter Novak, which first opened your mind to the latter question, was one of those flashes of insight that are themselves worth more as new questions than they are as answers, for his scheme never questioned that you are the individuals you seem, yet he described, and very well, the intellectual and spiritual emptiness that resulted from people having an inadequate conceptual description of their relationship to life after the body.)

Now let us look at what we have been describing as threads. And, as a note on the process, you might quote what Rita Warren told you.

Rita said that if, in order to understand A, you have to first understand B, but in order to understand B, you have to first understand A, all you can do is to keep approaching the subject, correcting previous misunderstandings or deepening your insights as each successive thing gets cleared up. Thus, you have to go through a series of wrong understandings, not because anyone wants to deceive you but because that's the only way you can build the necessary scaffolding, which then gets discarded in favor of new scaffolding which is still not right, but is at least farther along.

So imagine the job of teaching in such a circumstance, and

you will see why we are always playing your song, Frank—"But it's not that simple!"

We introduced the concept of threads as a way of loosening the hold on you of the idea that each person is an individual, in a way that each bit of salt in a salt shaker seems to be individual no matter how many granules there are. The old analogy of atoms—bits of irreducible substance, the "ultimate particles" that material existence *had to have* if the materialist worldview were correct—has carried much deeper into your mental and emotional world than you usually suspect. No one in medieval times (no matter how educated; it is not a matter of ignorance or simplicity) would have thought of himself as an isolated individual, still less as meaningless or the product of chance (which is saying the same thing twice). The medieval worldview *assumed* that all of creation lived within the creator. Your day's worldview assumes that you are all separate individuals rattling around, bumping together, struggling to get through a meaningless life. And your times have been unable to find a way from their "scientific" worldview into any intellectually respectable worldview that necessitates meaning and individual participation. Many are trying, with different parts of the puzzle. Those postulating that consciousness is primary are making headway, but perhaps you can see that this unconsidered assumption of individuality is the Trojan Horse they bring within their walls.

In order to loosen the idea of you as individuals, we had to start somewhere. So we said the invisible threads that connect you are as obvious to us as the containers that hold them. Now perhaps you will be able to see the threads as more primary than the rings. For, after all, traits are universal; individuals are transitory. Plato's categories—"chair-ness" for instance, though that was not necessarily one of his—were attempts to bring esoteric knowledge into a more widespread mental world. Devoid of context, how well could it be conveyed undistorted? How useful could it be?

But "threads" is a relatively static, relatively barren concept.

It is an intermediary, one more way of re-envisioning A. So now let us complicate it a bit, and perhaps give it more life even as an analogy, and see if we cannot inch closer to understanding both A and B. Of course, it is still going to be an analogy, but the point of analogy is not to paint a pretty picture but to say one thing that resonates, so that any given person's guidance can hold up an idea and have a better chance of being heeded.

We have spoken of threads, and sometimes of strings, ropes, and cables, meaning to loosely indicate that there are different levels of intensity. Some combinations are more likely to last, to have an effect, and are themselves inherently more meaningful. To have red hair by it self is after all only a matter of coloring. But if red hair is always or usually or even often accompanied by emotional volatility, you have the making of a more meaningful indicator.

However, so far this is still much too mechanical and lifeless, even though we are couching the discussion in terms of human traits such as temper or creativity. It's time to change the analogy from threads to something more interactive. *Bear in mind, this does not obviate the usefulness of the threads-and-containers analogy*; it merely uses whatever mental ground that analogy has gained, to proceed beyond it. This is what always must happen, if a concept is not to become an idol. It was necessary scaffolding and will continue to be so for others for whatever time they can use it, but it is scaffolding nonetheless, obscuring what it attempts to reveal.

Genetic Heredity

The rings-and-threads analogy was meant to loosen your prevailing model of individual-as-unit. There might have been other ways to do it—other analogies that would have worked—but this one seemed safest in part *because of* its limitations. If it had seemed more complete, more satisfying in itself, it might have been difficult to pry you away from it when the time came. Thus other cultures have had the same functions and structures described in terms more obviously alive, and people mistook concepts, abstractions, for reality in the sense of it being the only way to see things. Thus, spirit possession, for one example only. It's easier by far to move on from ring-and-threads because it is so clearly only an analogy. But that doesn't guarantee that it's going to be easy to get to a new place and still remember that it is only *one* way of seeing things.

To strip that analogy down to basics, you could say it concentrates on the connections *between* what seem to be units, rather than the connections *within* what seems to be units. But once you realize that you may be considered a person-group federating into social-groups, the seemingly absolute boundaries reveal themselves as more permeable, and little-noticed connections become seen in closer to their true importance.

So. You as individual are the physical heir to two sets of physical characteristics from your parents (and from them back to Adam and Eve, though there are practical limits to how far traits are inherited). Since there is no such thing as a purely physical trait, this means that you as constituted comprise a congeries of what could be looked at as intelligent beings that have learned over time to cooperate to different degrees.

The difficulty here continues to be the same one: The concept of individuality continually sneaks in through the back door. So let us begin from the other end and see where that takes us.

In a way, you as investigators into the true nature of your individuality are in much the same position as investigators into the ultimate constitution of matter. You could wind up looking for smaller and smaller "irreducible" particles, only to see each in turn recede as a prospect, as each proposed new "smallest unit" proves to be constituted of still smaller ones, or ones of another nature (as energy bundles rather than very small marbles). So we have talked of threads affiliating into strings, into ropes, into cables, extending the analogy but then being unable to make it meaningful beyond the very most elemental relationship. There isn't any way to move from cables, seen as an image, to the community—call it a person-group—you experience yourselves as. And if we try to build things up from traits, as if a couple of traits decided to combine, and gradually acquired a following and began operating as more complicated strings, or ropes, or whatever well, you can see the difficulty. You can recognize, now, that you are not a unit that is in any way indivisible, seen over time, seen in space, seen mentally—which means non-physically—or spiritually, which we will discuss some other time. So how to approach the question without silently postulating an "ultimate particle of matter," so to speak, or leaving the composition and even the origin of traits up in the air, unconnected to other things? The only way we can see to approach it is to begin from behavior and your common experience, so that we don't just create a pretty but ungrounded metaphor.

Heredity is one potential limitation of possibilities. If nowhere in your genetic structure was there any of the traits needed to be a successful Mozart, you wouldn't need to worry about becoming one. And this bears explaining, in that we have said that each of your parents' contributions to your physical heredity goes back to the beginnings of humanity. That is true in a way, and essentially not true in another way.

For all *practical* purposes, your hereditary traits go back only so far, because any trait by itself (i.e., not reinforced by other contributors of the same trait) must be lost. One half of each parent's characteristics are passed on in each child. Not necessarily the same half, of course, but half. One quarter of each grandparents', and one eighth of each grandparents' parents'. Seven generations winnow 128 sets of contributions down to one. But that is not the end, for each generation is itself a sifting process. That is, how you live determines to a degree which members of your person-group will be passed on enhanced, and which enfeebled or unchanged.

It should be obvious that here we deal with more than the composition of the parents at the time of conception of the child. Their subsequent life affects the child's heredity *in effect*, by, as it were, participating in the on-going debate, or jockeying for position, among the child's person-group.

In any given life, there are some things fixed—time and place of birth, birth order within family, etc.—and some things fluid, and some things that might be called something between fixed and fluid. This too is a topic apart, but notice: Your life— as we have emphasized from the beginning—is shaped by your choices, and is created specifically to allow and express those choices, and then to present further choices from those you already made. Until now we have emphasized choice in relation to the mind you are creating on an on-going basis, and that mind's function on the non-physical side after death.

Now we present another aspect. Your choices also help shape possibilities in time, for the time line downstream of you, so to speak. Your choices in life determine what further choices will become available to you; but they also determine what choices will become available to your genetic and your contemporary posterity. And that will take some explaining.

Perhaps it would be as correct to say they determine which choices will be *foreclosed*, or *prevented*, or *pre-empted*. In that sense, choice could be looked at as a continuing winnowing, a non-stop process of attrition from the stock remaining—a process of attrition compensated for by the continual presentation of new possibilities. But surely it can be seen that the winnowing process tends to limit the *quality* of what new elements are received. If you keep discarding artistic expression, let's say, then fewer such possibilities will be presented as viable options. You don't get to Carnegie Hall without practicing, and at some point—perhaps quite an early point—it becomes too late to overcome the gap between what you need to have done and what you have done. When you are 30, you can't be retroactively different at 20, in any given time-line.

We don't need to continue on the subject of genetics and heredity, once the point has been grasped. Genetics is a set of physical limitations. Others exist. You may remember that some while ago we said that often enough we had to make do, in the shaping of a person, because the best combination nevertheless included some traits we wished weren't there. In other words, in any given situation one takes the best *possible* combination. Not necessarily the best conceivable, but the best among those available. Genius results, often enough, when very different genetic backgrounds are mixed. Talent often enough is produced by successive generations of similar backgrounds continuing to interact. The former—William Butler Yeats. The latter—the musical family of Bachs.

The Software of the Individual

Physical heredity acts as much as a negative as a positive. That is, it determines what kinds of things *can't* come in, as well as (in the same process, as part of the same reality as) what *can*. You might look at your physical heredity as the software running on the hardware of the physical base.

The specific genetics of a given individual could be considered to be the software, running on the firmware of the human pattern, running on the hardware of cellular matter. Looked at this way, your physical heredity is not exactly the physical body but the shape, the specific nature, of your particular body.

Given that the firmware is the human form, the software running on that firmware is the individual's particular possibilities. You might say that on the human firmware are all those millions of programs that have been developed, subset after subset, specialized application after specialized application, more complex as time goes on, as the software itself has a built-in learning capacity. We won't stop to do the work, but you could do it easily enough, any of you. First male or female, the very primary division. Then within that, the various emotional and chemical variations of male and female. Then all the innumerable polarities and positions on the scale between all those polarities, the result being perhaps millions of possible combinations. On that software base one then runs data—and that data is what you bring to the mixture of traits that is your heredity.

Now, bear in mind, the software shaping the individual (by selecting among possibilities) is *aware* of the data to be run. This is in no way a matter of chance. All those winnowings of firmware-constrained possibilities—vast enough, after all—still leave huge amounts of significant traits and combinations of traits to be chosen among. Your physical ancestry is a limited vocabulary of choices—but *limited* is not the same as *few*. It isn't like your genetic heritage determines what you must be. It doesn't. It determines what the limits are of the pool from which you must be chosen.

This is a vitally important point, though it seems simple enough to us. Nothing in your family history determines that you *must* have red hair, or be left-handed, or have an equable temper, or be scientifically inclined, or have an ungovernable aversion to snakes, or be afflicted by tuberculosis or even have a "hereditary" predisposition to contract it. Those are all *possibilities*! They are not limitations or requirements or something predestined. Your software contains a limited but hardly scant array of possibilities from which *you* are assembled, or gravitate, however you wish to put it. But there is no reliance on chance in the choosing, except in the inessentials. (Your life's purpose may not have anything to do with your favorite color, or your attitude toward cats, or even your interaction with your relations. It *may*. Or it may not.)

Well, obviously if your software provides the range of choices, and the choices are made with an end in mind (that is, with the construction of an individual to fit into certain circumstances and to function in certain ways that may not even exist as yet) *someone* or *something* informs those choices, according to some criteria that may be looked at as a life-plan or an experiment or some other idea. The only alternative is to believe that the individual is shaped by chance, and from that it is a short path to deciding that all of life is chance, hence meaningless or illusionary or inscrutable. Yet your experiences, once you delve a little beneath the surface, convince you easily that there's something vastly more interesting going on, vastly more meaningful and structured, than chance. This is the factor that is introduced as what we might call your spiritual heredity, and it is the invisibility of this factor to a certain mentality that leads it to conclude that life is chance (hence, meaningless). For in the absence of a concept such as we are attempting to provide, one's only intellectual choice is to concede some variation of the statement, "God made me," and while we don't have a particular aversion to that attitude, we recognize that for many people it is an unconquerable obstacle. We also recognize that it isn't particularly helpful in making sense of life unless one can accept the rest of the God-centered attitude, for otherwise one winds up with an ungrounded concept contradicting the rest of the assumptions and interpretations that comprise one's mental existence. *[Chapter Three discusses the concept of God as creator.]*

Spiritual Heredity

But although genetic heritage is one set of constraints, or one set of possibilities made manifest, it is not the only one. One's physical heredity is the container. Into it, one pours one's own contents, one's spiritual heredity.

What we think of as past lives.

What you somewhat loosely think of as past lives, yes—for usually the concept and practice rests upon the assumption of individuality somewhere with you the irreducible atom, well disguised, and therefore "you" are moving from life to life, like discarding and picking up costumes, or changing roles. Once you take into account the differences in genetic heredity lifetime to lifetime, this view appears to be a little shallow, for it assumes that the traveling soul is realer than its various manifestations in life. This is the view that sees life on earth as meaningless distraction, as illusion, and sees the physical world as maya.

Perhaps we should go into that view in greater depth. But perhaps it isn't necessary or productive. Buddhism isn't wrong in seeing the physical life as less meaningful than it appears—but it isn't absolutely right either, for the soul's journeys are more than distractions and illusion. Reality is not just an endless school for the education of ignorant beings.

I have this argument every so often. So many people talk of the earth-school, and they see our task as living to learn lessons. They think that life is spirit, or consciousness, inserting itself into unconscious matter, we observing and participating in the process.

We have been encouraging you away from that belief as we earlier encouraged you away from the belief that life is meaningless, or that life is any given definition of life. "Words are a prison. God is free," expresses the un-capture-able nature of life, negative though its conclusions must necessarily be in those circumstances.

A problem with any attempt to make sense of life—including this one—is that the situation appears different depending on what aspect of it one examines. Every answer any sincere seeker has ever obtained is true *to a degree*, and *within a given set of circumstances*, or, one might say, *from a certain point of view*. You will remember that some years ago, when we were asked for effective exercises to improve one's spirituality, we gave as one such exercise practicing changing points of view. That was recommended with the idea of helping you see differently. As we said at the time, it doesn't *seem* to have anything to do with the matter of spirituality, yet it may help bring one to the attitude, the stance, that will make it possible to see things differently, which is all that "spirituality" is, really. So, to say that life as you experience it is largely illusion is true, but it is also true that your life has real consequences, for you and for others.

Works in Progress

Your consciousness as it exists—that is, what you have available to work with, moment by moment—is neither stable nor uniform nor consistent nor self-aware. If you had your person-group—your various active threads—welded into a unit, or (to use a more biological analogy) functioning as a team under your continuous awareness, your experience of consciousness would be a very different thing, and you would be—will be—in effect a different, more effective, more fulfilled, person, with greater potential opening up as you gained greater control. As it is, you function haltingly, partly paralyzed, scarcely a unit in function at all.

This is not the fault of *moral flaws*, and therefore cannot be corrected by moral laws or attempts at "self-improvement." (Such attempts will have their own effects and rewards, but not this one.)

It is not the result of *ignorance*, and therefore cannot be corrected by the acquisition of knowledge. (The acquisition of knowledge may be good in itself—including the perception of the nature of good and evil, for instance—but can only act as catalyst, at best.)

It is not the result of *karma* in the sense of paying for past sins, (though we can see how it may look that way, in that as you judge your progress you say to yourself, "if I had been born as a better package I'd be further ahead." This is entirely incorrect and at any rate irrelevant. Your aunt, not having wheels, is not a tea cart.)

Least of all is it the result of *chance*, which plays no part in any meaningful way.

It is because you are a work in progress, as are we, and as are each of your constituent parts. See it thus:

1. *Group-mind:* the consciousness of the higher group—your guys upstairs—of which you as a person-group are one strand.

2. *Person-mind:* the consciousness you experience day-to-day as a person-group.

3. *Strand-mind:* the consciousness of the lower-level person-group that seems to you only a strand in your web.

This creation of a specialized jargon is in a way regrettable, but cannot be avoided if we are to pack enough concept into symbol to continue your education. Thus, to re-state: Your person-mind is a work in progress, as is our group-mind, and each strand-mind. Everything is alive and moving and everything affects everything else (there being no "units," but only one thing). As the consciousness of any one level fluctuates, so everything it connects to is affected; and so reciprocally.

You come into life to be the ring-master of many elements, each of which is itself in the process of continuous flux in the same way and for the same reason. Does this not shed light on why life is so complex and continuously changing? It isn't just a matter of astrology, of different celestial influences on an otherwise unchanging individual. It isn't just sociology, a matter of the patterns set up around you by your environment. And it isn't just psychology, between the two, a matter of mind in an environment, although this is closest. It is as common sense would suppose, only the unit is vastly more porous than is commonly supposed.

Remember always—perhaps we don't stress this strongly enough or often enough—it isn't that we are providing you with new material as much as a new way of putting together the pieces. So you will find bits in Seth or in Gurdjieff or anywhere and suddenly you will see what was being said that you couldn't, previously, ground in your life. And of course it will work the other way, as well. Something another body of information offers will explain what we provide here.

Now, you are in a body as ring-master of all these elements, aware of them to greater or lesser extent. At one level of consciousness all things seem part of you and you of them, and no meaningful separation presents itself. This is the infant before it forms an "I" relative to the rest of the world—and it is the individual awareness *after* it has gone through the perception of separation between the I and the other—more or less what you're getting to now, conceptually. In the long meantime, your relationship with all those elements varies all over the place. Sometimes you are not very aware of forces beyond your definition of your consciousness and other times you are more so. (Besides fluctuations within any one person, there are wide variations between individuals, as should be obvious. Some at their most sensitive to other influences are not nearly as sensitive as others at their least sensitive. Each person-group differs from others in this, as in other things.)

A person's actions, thoughts, reactions, may be as baffling to the person-group itself as to any others. What you do in life is not necessarily about what you think or assume or hope it is. There is so much going on behind the scenes! Is it a wonder that you sometimes awaken from a dream and wonder what you've been doing? But some people can live more comfortably knowing more, others, more comfortably knowing less. And—like the hired man Tarbox who said it to Emerson as a young man, that you like to quote occasionally—"people are always praying, and their prayers are always answered." You get out of life what the person-group really wants. The difficulty is that what the person-group wants and needs may be very different from what the volatile consciousness that is trying to coordinate the group (what you may call the ego) wants.

Many Lives Within a Life

There is a *logic* behind your existence in any particular body at any particular time-and-place. Now listen carefully to the end of that statement. The logic changes according to the time, according to the place. That's why you change locations or change occupations or change *pre*occupations. You live many lives within any given life—as child, as adolescent, as young relatively irresponsible adult, as functioning social unit primarily driven by the needs and motivations of the larger society around you, as older person with a longer perspective, as—perhaps, elder, either known for wisdom or ignored as irrelevant. All this is familiar to you from a *social* viewpoint. Now think of it from an internal or spiritual viewpoint. You live many lives within each life. *Why* is that? *How* is that?

Of course you will see that part of the answer is that your person-group expresses different constituent parts in different circumstances—including the chronologically-biologically determined circumstances you think of as different stages of life. It should be easily comprehensible that throughout your lifetime you are necessarily different persons. That is, different aspects manifest in turn, and not necessarily once and then not again. You have heard of terms like "arrested development" or "reversion to an earlier form" but may not have considered them in this context.

How different is it when you consider your larger existence? Suppose yourself a being with many threads each of which, or each combination of which, expresses at different times in different circumstances. How different is that from your present circumstances? As above, so below.

Okay, big jump but I see it. The common thread in our lives is not so much the body (except at any given moment) but the mind, the consciousness, that somehow has both the moment-to-moment consciousness (and ignorance) and the overview of the life.

Nice jump. Yes. As above, so below, because each level is the same scheme, the same pattern, as the level below or above, and so understanding one's own level is the way to understand all other levels. And after all, how else could you—how could the ancients, how could the wisdom-keepers—obtain first-hand knowledge of other levels of being? (This doesn't mean that everything that is experienced is understood in the same way; it *does* mean, though, that it is the same thing being experienced. Thus, with sufficient insight, one can examine any testimony, correct for its bias, and see the same thing as it appeared from a different viewpoint.)

In any given life, there are stages of growth, times of decay, sudden discontinuities, bewildering crosscurrents. There are strong influences from others, pleasant or unpleasant or alternatingly pleasant and unpleasant or combined intense pleasant-unpleasant flavors. You have intellectual "abstract" interests, artistic "aesthetic" appreciations, strong and weak emotions, satisfactions that are not easily classified. You learn skills, you endure hardships, you—in short—experience life. Now, what happens during this experiencing of life? Our scheme consists of person-groups cohabiting a bodily locus and so experiencing a day-by-day identification with each other, strong or weak or unwilling or unaware, just as you do with external society and for the same reason, because the nature of "inside" and "outside" is the same.

So, at one stage of life any given combination of traits may be—activated, let's call it. Evoked. Exercised. Experienced. Relied upon. Developed. At another stage of life, another combination takes the stage (so to speak) and this combination may have little or no or much or conceivably even almost entire continuity with the previous combination, hence "you" change to meet new circumstances. If you were describing just the same process, but were considering it in terms of "reincarnation" as it is called, can you see that it's the same process? If you as an "individual" should really be seen as a person-group consisting of many strands, can you see that your particular person-group may be seen as one strand in a many-lived person-group? And so up and down the scale?

We'll hammer that home a little, though it will be evident to some.

Your "higher self" and your mind are not exactly the same thing seen in different contexts. Your mind, your mental world, is non-physical, yes. But just because your higher self is also non-physical does not mean it is the same as your mind, any more than the fact that your physical body is physical means it is indistinguishable from a chicken.

Vertical Integration

The next analogy to consider is at a lower level. Just as it is true that a person-group may be considered one thread of a larger organism, [which is] a person-group of its own, so it is true that each thread—each trait—of your own may be considered a person-group of its own at a lower level. And of course all of this will need to be spelled out—or hinted at, really, as we must proceed mostly by analogy. It remains true that we are attempting to convey information that cannot be expressed directly in words.

We suggest that you provide a sketch, incorporating your understanding of what we're saying here, to show:

• the composition of any given "individual."

- the vertical integration of one layer with another above or below it

- the composition of any of those layers, as well.

Now, notice how hard it is to really grasp the meaning of so abstract a statement, yet how it seems to bring things almost into view. Consider an abstract statement to be a road map, good primarily for indicating relationships but not good at much else. If you already know any of the territory, it may remind you. If you do not, it can't give you the idea. So the thing to do is to use an abstract statement as it is meant to be used. First, as an orienting device, then— *after you've been to the territory*—as a reminder, as a way to integrate what you have newly seen with what you knew beforehand.

This is a way of saying that abstractions must be alternated with something that will engage your emotional bodies, not only your mental bodies. That's why we alternate abstraction and analogy. Thus, if we accustom you to see yourselves as a person-group rather than as a unit, we can *then* proceed to tie that understanding to new abstraction. But until we had illustrated it in ways that lead you to be able to relate it to the rest of your lives, we couldn't have done much with it. This is why this tutelage proceeds so slowly *and* so discursively. It isn't our whim or Frank's; it is a teaching method, and a preference.

So if a person-group, taken as a whole, functioning as a unit, may be considered to be as one strand in a larger unit, equally may each strand in your lives be taken as a person-group in its own right, and that strand—that person-group—may be considered to be itself a complex group of strands functioning temporarily as a unit.

Can we say it any plainer? We will try. We do recognize that our careful habit of using qualifiers and modifiers may impede clarity. So the skeleton is: As above, so below.

As Above, So Below

You've often heard it, but have you ever understood what you were hearing? How could you, in the absence of explanation? Yet how could the explanation be given to anyone who clung to the "obvious" accepted explanations of life? If "common sense" is your guide, you will never get beyond it to any uncommon sense. Think how long a trail to get to so simple an explanation.

Every layer of reality is, in the first place, not a "level" at all, in the sense of a different discrete "place" or stage. A level is merely a part of reality temporarily considered out of context. The fact that it is studied out of context does not mean that those particular facts belong together more than they belong to the context from which they were (temporarily, provisionally) ripped. It is merely a necessity, a convenience, to consider them in isolation so that they may be given a label and considered as one. So—you as person-groups. You are not in any way separate from your constituent parts, nor from the larger context that you are part of. It is merely that for the purpose of analysis it is usually convenient to consider certain relationships in isolation from their vertical (so to speak) associations.

Anything held in isolation is thereby distorted. The distortion is unavoidable given the limitations of mind functioning in time-space, but it must be noted. To study *anything* is to study it somewhat in isolation from factors that are important to its understanding. Just remember that, or try to come back to it, anyway.

The fact that a given set of phenomena, closely linked, are usually or always considered together will mean that your minds will tend to make into units what are only parts of the flow. Necessary for understanding, but necessarily producing *mis*understanding, in the process.

What we are getting to, since you ask, is this. Although we, and you, are accustomed to thinking in "layers," that is merely because it is easiest to slice reality that way. But it can as easily be sliced in other ways, and you do so when, for instance, you consider physical versus non-physical. In that mental association-set, you take every physical manifestation from the smallest so-called atom to the largest physical manifestation you can think of—galaxies, universes—and disregard for the moment the divisions that otherwise seem so important and real to you. For that moment, the physical world is seen, dimly, as all one thing. But of course even the division between physical and non-physical is a *created* division, a perception of a relative difference made more absolute than it really is.

In pointing out that reality doesn't really separate in the way it is convenient for us to analyze it, we don't intend to therefore throw up our non-physical hands and give up trying to explain. We are merely bookmarking the fact that there's a difference between structure and scaffolding.

So, to descend. Within you as person-groups are what seem like past-life traits and knowledge. But how can that be, when these past lives are also seen as part of a higher-layer being of which *you* are but a strand? Can a thing be both smaller and larger than you? (Yes, of course "smaller" and "larger" are only physical analogies, but you get the idea, so they serve the purpose.)

Or, moving upward, can something separate from you (for that is how another life feels, is it not?) be at the same time a part of you, so that the entire "unit" that is a past life is only a part of you, yet you as "unit" are only a part of it?

The very inexplicability of the situation—inexplicable by logical development, we mean—is what drove and drives so many explorers to say that it cannot be expressed. And yet, once you get the sense of it, thumbnail expressions such as "as above, so below" are able to remind you of relationships understood, and suggest to you an extension of these relationships. A mystery-school's mysteries had to be kept secret not lest the general populace would understand but *because* they *couldn't*. Think what a mystery school's contents did, released to the public as an emotional story.

Christianity, you mean.

Certainly. Jesus expressed profound truths and did so in parables—as religions are always forced to do—so that he could at the same time say what was true, for those who could hear, and say what was helpful even though it would be misunderstood, for those who couldn't. Yet anyone who came to be a part of the Christian religion came to assume that the inner truths Jesus taught were understood by them ex officio as Catholics, so to speak, or ex officio, later, as Protestants listening for the direct voice of God. It has become necessary to destroy the shell of Christianity in order that new life could arise from its ashes (to mix metaphors) but that doesn't mean that it didn't embody the truth. It did, but the truth could not be understood by people at a common level of being no matter how acute their intellects or how fervent their faith.

The situation is no different today with the religion of scientism. There's a very good reason for not worshiping idols, and it has nothing to do with the jealousy of an almighty creator, and everything to do with the distortion that results from seeing things in wrong proportion, wrong context.

Three Levels

I have just spent half an hour or so reviewing the material given, and I am a bit staggered by the amount of new information, new ways of seeing things, that you have provided, so smoothly and quietly. Once I absorbed it, it's now so obvious-seeming.

In that, you see the benefits of sending this out *[to friends on the Internet]* in real time—day by day—and getting feedback from this or that person as you go along. The interchange, the suggested ideas, even the misunderstandings, are all productive. So, last night you were given two. Do you remember both?

With your assistance, I imagine I will. One is that the various strands that comprise our person-groups are not units themselves (as you said earlier) and therefore are not, within themselves, at any uniform level of development. Another is, neither are we.

Yes, and of course both points are obvious as soon as you remember that as it is above, so it is below. You experience yourselves as comprising elements some of which lead you "upward" and others of which lead you "downward"—that is, toward or away from whatever value we may be considering at any given moment. Some are "good" habits, some are "bad" habits. Hemingway, for instance, was a careful and meticulous craftsman, clearly a good trait, except he was at the same time an exacting and intolerant man in his judgment of others. You see—because of how we just set it up—that these are merely exterior judgments of the same sort of trait expressed in different contexts. Painstaking craftsmanship *is*, in a curious way, a form of intolerance, only seen differently.

Now, hold that thought and consider that what you are used to calling traits are in fact person-groups in themselves, and you can see perhaps that the same trait is going to express differently in different contexts according to how different strands *within it* are evoked by what it can only see as external circumstances. Thus, the person-group responsible for craftsmanship may be the same person-group responsible for any other irrationally obsessive behavior. ("Irrationally" meaning, here, not the result of consciousness or decision but functioning more or less autonomously.)

Again, as above, so below. Take your own lives (because experienced from the inside) or take Hemingway's life (because partly expressed in his writing, and partly recounted in biographies, and partly explored herein along with him in a sort of inside-but-outside view). Try *applying* these concepts so that you can work out how they function in real life, and so that your own access to higher levels of your person-group may provide you with insight as you focus.

Wow, I got a real glimpse of many things as we wrote that! I hope you're making notes as we go!

The more you *work* the material, the more you will thereby unpack what is contained within it. You just got a glimpse, or perhaps we should call it an intuitive knowing—same thing, really—of how you function upward, in analogy to how your lesser levels function in relation to you.

And I almost see how a thing can be smaller than us and larger than us at the same time.

If the spatial analogy did not so consistently obtrude, the misunderstanding would not exist. Try to explain; we will correct as needed, but the effort of explaining renders material of any sort more accessible to you; it makes it yours by tying it in.

It is (I think) the threads analogy that just gave it to me. And as I start to write this I see again that the old strings-and-rings analogy is being changed on me as I go along, or perhaps I never understood it in a way it was also meant. I thought of it as expressing the interconnecting of various individuals by shared traits, but that was before I realized that at all "levels" we are not units but—squads, say. That isn't wrong, but it isn't enough. I don't know that I know quite how to clarify (even to myself, not merely to others) this new context.

Instead of thinking of a strand as a strand, a thread as a thread, you could perhaps look at things this way, in three "levels":

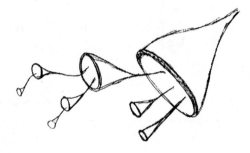

[Again using my sketch: From left to right, strand-mind, person-mind, group-mind.]

Which "level" is "real," or "complete" or more integral? Which is the "correct" viewpoint from which to judge other levels?

Clearly, wherever you are situated.

Of course, because you never have a choice in the matter. *Everything* is relative to everything else, so why bother to look elsewhere for a better place from which to judge? The only reason to envision changing viewpoint places is to provide binocular rather than monocular vision. But it remains true that "man is the measure of all things." This is true at the level of person-group "above" or "below" you as well—or didn't you ever stop to think that any consciousness is as real to it as yours is to you?

Well, when I do healing work through communication with the body part, or with the internal personality considered as robot, I talk to it just as to any other person.

Yes—often somewhat to their surprise, though you haven't realized it. To them the sudden transparency of the veil between your level and theirs is as startling as yours, initially, when talking to us across the veil that you took to be between physical and non-physical.

Hadn't made that connection. Of course, if mind is non-physical, that wasn't the veil involved, was it?

[And this brings us to the question of the physical and the non-physical, and how they interact. Life absolutely cannot be understood except as a complex, continuing interaction between the physical and the non-physical. And it is to that relationship that we now turn.]

Chapter Three

The Physical and the Non-Physical

If you realized that the nurtured spiritual part of yourself would accompany you on your eternal journey and that everything else you have labored so hard to accumulate would vanish the instant you depart this world, would it alter your daily agenda?
—Walter Cooper, *Shards: Restoring the Shattered Spirit*

If you think you came into being for the purpose of taking an important part in the administration of events, to guard a province of the moral creation from ruin, and that its salvation hinges on the success of your single arm, you have wholly mistaken your business.
—Emerson in his journal, 1828, age 25

Why Does the World Exist?

[Sitting with my journal one morning, I summarized what I understood of what the guys had told me to date, then (in italics) moved to direct interaction.]

Some years ago, a friend asked me to ask the guys upstairs why we are here and what life is all about. The beginnings of an answer to that question lie in the nature and interrelationship of the physical and non-physical worlds. We know that physical exists, because we live here. Even if physical reality is *ultimately* an illusion, or if (as is very likely) its true nature is quite different from our ideas of it, anyway we know it's here and we know that it is an integral part of the non-physical world. But when we try to think about the interaction of the physical and the non-physical world, the spatial analogy sneaks into all our ideas and distorts them. Thus we think of the physical as being "here" and the non-physical being "there." But it isn't "there"; it is here, in the only "here" there is. I think of the non-physical world as vibrating at a higher frequency than the physical world (an analogy, remember), thus in a way being both here and not-quite-here. Perhaps this is why the two worlds sometimes seem to overlap, and we know or experience things that we shouldn't be able to. We in the physical can't experience the non-physical with our senses but we can experience it otherwise. And if we can remember that what I call "the other side"—the non-physical world—it is *right here,* we eliminate or minimize one source of error, the spatial analogy.

I suspect that it's time for a word from our sponsors. How'd I do so far?

You show a pretty good working understanding of what we have been telling you. You haven't mentioned delayed consequences as a sort of explanatory device—making sure you absorb the results of various decisions, you know—but otherwise unexceptionable. Still your question remains: *Why* do you do this; why does the universe exist; why is there a God or a box of corn flakes, and what are they to you. You used to say that you in physical are in the position of a fish at the bottom of the sea trying to imagine a man on the top of a mountain watching television. Nice analogy, and still true.

"Why is there air," Bill Cosby used to ask as part of a comedy routine. Nothing wrong with asking the question, as long as you remember (or realize in the first place!) that there can be no answer divorced from the interests of the questioner. "To blow basketballs up with" is logical, accurate, and germane, if that is where your interests lie. "To provide an exchange medium for plants and animals" would be equally true—*but no more true*, merely from a wider perspective. "Why" is a question whose answer is always improvised according to the nature of the person responding. In our view "why" does not rank with "how." You may never know *why* you live, but you probably should give thought to *how*. Naturally the two questions are related, but either question is more meaningful in connection to the other than standing alone; that is why we bring "how" into the discussion.

Space, Time, and the Illusion of Separation

Space produces the illusion of separation, of individuality, of non-belonging, of difference, in a way that would not be possible otherwise. And if space produces the illusion of separation, time produces the effect of delayed consequences. Time, in the way you experience it, sorts out everything just as space does. Last Tuesday is so definitely different from a given date three years ago that you could (and do) stack different people and things in the same space and different time and not have them collide. Time, like space, sorts out the world around you. But they are experienced radically differently: You are not frog-marched through space, inch by inch by inch, always in one direction. But you *are* frog-marched through time. At least, that's how you experience it. But your interpretation of your experience misleads you.

When a moment of time "passes"—that moment does not cease to exist: *You* cease to exist *in it*. *You* have been carried smoothly to the next moment of time. If you are standing still for five such moments, it looks to you that you moved in time and not in space. But it could equally truly be said that you moved in time-space. That is, moment one exists next to moment two, and you moved from one to two. Then you moved to moment three, then four—and your movement is continuous, predictable and not under your control, so when you get to moment five you assume that the "previous"—which really means previously experienced—moments have somehow ceased to exist.

Your experience tells you that moving through time is like hopping from ice-floe to ice-floe to get across the river, with each previous ice-floe ceasing to exist as soon as you jump from it, and—even more startling, more hazardous—the next ice floe not even coming into existence until you land on it! You never can pause, nor can you do a thing about the situation except to jump in one direction rather than another. If you wanted to rest at any given floe you couldn't, not only because you don't know how to do it, but because what would you do when the floe ceases to exist in the next moment?

What a situation! If it were a true description, you'd be in a pretty bad fix—and, we know, this is how many of you *do* experience your lives. But there's a better way to see it, that will relieve the insecurity. The ice-floe you are standing on does not cease to exist just because you jump from it (or, to put it more closely, are smoothly catapulted from it). And icebergs "to come" are not as-yet-uncreated but already exist, just as they would in a physical-geography metaphor. (Disregard for the moment the fact that you can't see how that could be: Hold the theoretical possibility. All you are doing is creating a space in your mind for a new way of seeing things.)

People who say we have "no time" on "this side" mean by that (though they often do not *know* what they mean) that we are not subject to that unvarying tyranny, moving us along. That is sort of true, in the same way that it is sort of true that we have no space. *Neither statement is true* except in reference to your experience. We have time, we have space—how else could we structure experience? But they are not what they seem to you to be. They are neither prisons nor constrictions—but they are real limitations. Try to envision a life without limitations and you will end up with fog. *It is the same world.* Canada—the physical Canada—exists "here" as it does "there," because we are not someplace else! The non-physical components of the physical world are—right here! Why would you think they are elsewhere? It isn't even true that you cannot perceive it; it is true only that you cannot perceive it in the same way or using the same faculties that you do the physical world—we might almost say *the rest of* the physical world.

We know that this is a radically different thought for many, so we will try to say it carefully. The non-physical world is right "there" with you, and right "then" with you. How far do you think it is from Baltimore to the non-physical equivalent of Baltimore? And why would you think that the physical Baltimore doesn't have its non-physical equivalent? What do you think you build on earth, anyway? But because you misunderstand time, you think that things "pass away" on earth (and presumably in the non-physical earth). Not true in either case.

Where is ancient Rome, say March 1, 250 b.c.? That world on that day is where it always was and always will be. We on this side can "go" there at will; you on your side cannot (normally). And so we on our side we do not get bored, and you on your side get to play with greater consequences. This is the chief difference between our experience of the world and yours. It is a simple concept, but foreign to your usual ways of understanding. We are trying to express it in simple terms devoid of jargon.

Now we are doing quite a bit of hopping ourselves! We are touching on this, touching on that, and not tying up anything. But it is necessary to present several ideas before we can create a model. Continued patience, please.

It is the nature of the physical world—and by "world" we mean not one planet but all of physical creation—to lead its inhabitants to experience one time, one space, then movement to another time, and perhaps to another place. *Spatially* you may move forward, back, right, left, up, down. To Cleveland, to Greenland, to Mars, wherever. The only restrictions on movement are obstacles such as distance, or the nature of the terrain, or whatever. Overcome the obstacle and you may move there. *Temporally*, however, you may move and must move in only one direction—"forward"—and you seemingly cannot vary the speed or direction in which you are carried. In fact, *because* you are carried, it seems to you that you have no control whatever over your movement in time. Now, that is a fair representation, is it not, of your plight on earth? Freedom in three dimensions, no freedom—not even freedom to stop!—in the fourth. Not an incorrect model, but not a very helpful one either. Let us see if we can improve upon it.

We have said that "Canada exists" over here. By that we do not mean that we have a sort of Disneyland version of Canada for people to play pretend in. We mean—Canada here and Canada there are extensions of the same thing, just as you extend "over here" and we "over there." A continuing distortion in these discussions is that spatial and temporal analogies continually sneak in between the lines, because language as it exists reflects your concept of reality. If we were to drop your analogy of this side/ that side, we would still need to pick up another, which would have its own defects. That can be a good thing when an analogy has become constricting or very misleading—but until then, why not continue to elaborate on what we're building? It's just a matter of periodic reminders of the limitations of analogy.

Creation and Creator

Let's talk about God.

You have never been much willing to talk about God.

It is a contentious subject not only among others but within yourself (which distinction is a difference more of language than of reality, you know). The result is to make you really nervous when we come to speak of the subject, for part of you pulls this way, part that way, part doesn't want to move, and another part covers its ears and pretends to know nothing. Metaphorically speaking, of course, but truly.

Thus I have always had anxiety about whatever you might say about the subject.

More than that, in fact. You and others find yourself getting a little irritable, a little short, when someone voices an opinion about is there a God and if so what are God's attributes. It is one subject that is always taboo, or at any rate always hedged-round with great obstacles. Why do you suppose this is?

When I was writing that, I got that nobody can look the sun in the eye.

True enough too, but not our point here. The fact that people of different opinions—or opinions unknown to one another—can discuss the subject only with the very greatest of care (or with brutal overriding of the other party's opinions) should tell you something.

No doubt. But—what? That it's important to them, I suppose. But people are edgy over gun control, too, or abortion or other social issues.

Social issues define your opinions in terms of your values, so of course there is going to be strong identification. But God is the ultimate identifier. To believe in God or believe in no-God or believe in non-believing-either-way, is to define yourself in all other terms, for how you form your values . . . .

Well, let's go at it another way. We were going to make a

statement about how values are formed, but there's a difference between conscious processes and unconscious ones. Instead, we will say what we know of God.

We have told you many times that the fish is unlikely to have created the fishbowl, or the water that fills it. Without expressing an opinion of the nature of whatever created the fishbowl, clearly it wasn't the fish itself. So there is the first aspect—something created physical life.

Clearly it can only have been created out of something other than physical life, or we are only playing with words (and we are not). So, something non-physical created the physical. How it was done, and according to what laws—and, still less for the moment, *why* it was done—is not unarguable. What *is* beyond argument is that the created did not create itself.

Think for a moment of the complexity of a baby, and its helplessness. That baby was created out of the physical being of its parents, and is nurtured by their providing its requirements which they extract from their environment and render suitable for it.

Could that baby create itself "spontaneously"? Could it manifest the complex arrangement of complex systems of subsidiary, equally complex, systems? Could a baby even design itself, let alone maintain itself? Obviously not. Well, the universe is more complex than a baby. The job is harder, not easier, to create space-time and all its laws and substances. If it ever looks easier, it is because most of the complexity and the concatenation of complexity is hidden from you. Anything looks easy, from sufficient distance.

So let us say, something created the physical universe. Even if after that moment of initial architecture (setting rules and inter-relationships) no further intervention were required or possible, there had to be something outside of it to create it. If you were to find this statement emotionally unacceptable, there would be not much point in proceeding farther, for you would be reading it as though humoring us. (And this is the defensive posture people often enough find themselves drawn to, when the subject comes up. Even if they consciously, intellectually, wish to give the subject fair consideration, unconsciously, emotionally, they are being churned up to the point of being unable to quietly concentrate and consider. This is a case of robots in action— robots as in, unconscious mechanisms automatically and infallibly performing the same response to the same stimulus unless or until brought up short by consciousness and reprogrammed to allow just consideration.)

Once admit that *something* created the physical universe, and you are over the worst hurdle. You are no longer requiring yourself to try to believe in a self-creating something. That step may not seem to you to be so large, but consider. A universe that created itself could be considered to be a universe that came into being "spontaneously" or—in essence—accidentally. And how could an accidental universe have meaning? And within an accidental universe, how could your lives have meaning? The first hurdle is, *are you afraid to believe that life has meaning?* If so, then you will find yourself forced to believe (or rather, unable to disbelieve) that creation had no creator, because a creator implies a reason for creation, if only curiosity, if only play.

We omit the G-word. We say, for the moment, that the physical universe was created out of the non-physical, and it was created exhibiting certain characteristics, chiefly a bias toward the creation and destruction of orderly systems. It—and therefore every part of it—demonstrates, by what it is, characteristics presumably reflecting the non-material universe where it was created, as they manifest under the peculiar restraints of physical laws.

None of this says anything about any religion. It attributes no particular characteristics to the creator. It does not venture an opinion as to whether the creator is singular or plural, or whether creation is repeatedly affected by the creator after initial creation or not. We know more than we are saying for the moment. For the moment, we want to get one point across, and only one.

The physical universe was created out of the non-physical.

If this is too much for you to swallow, then, as we say, there is no point in your pretending to consider what follows. Any redefinition of the sentence above either amounts to sleight-of-hand or is without meaning.

If you can accept the first statement, a second follows: *The physical universe takes its essence from the non-physical*, including the laws of its existence such as polarity, motion, etc. That is, in being created, the laws of its nature were built-in. A thing's boundaries and possibilities are defined right into it, via the laws of its existence.

Such creation implies intelligence—awareness—on the part of the creator. As functioning airplanes do not arise as a result of a tornado in a junkyard (as has been said of human evolution), so it is with the creation of the physical universe itself. Any order within it was *inherent*, obviously. Inherent order may arise from the nature of the thing being ordered, but it does not arise undirected from chaos.

Another word on that, since it may not be clear. Chaos theory, a relatively new development of science, shows something of the complex interactivity, *inherent in* systems, between order and chaos. In other words, there is order within chaos and chaos within order. Both are built-in; each depends upon the other. That should tell you that, at a higher order of complexity, the chaos-order dance is one of the laws of creation.

In other words if you look closely enough, even chaos is only apparently chaotic.

True enough, but if you look closely enough even order is only apparently orderly, or ordered. Order-chaos is one of those polarities within which physical life is lived, and cannot be escaped any more than hot-cold or any other polarity.

Can we sum up?

It is not important what you believe of God but it is very important that you believe that the physical universe was created from the non-physical, and that it may have a purpose. We say "may have" merely to bring along those who are wary of committing themselves farther than they are ready to do. But if you are able to believe only in non-purpose—almost *anti*-purpose—because you think that is the only realistic non-romantic view to take of the world, there is no hope within you. We are merely pointing out that such a dismal view is, fortunately for life, totally unjustified.

I am aware that this leaves hanging the question of whether the non-physical world was created, and if so out of what and if not, then what.

Let the question hang unanswered. For *practical* purposes it is enough to realize that you live in a created material universe.

A Continuing Interaction

Outside physical time-space, minds exist in a more or less permanent form. What we on the non-physical side are, was shaped by what we did while in the body with the original inheritance we began from when we entered the physical. Within physical time-space, new minds—new "souls" in restricted sense—are formed with each new body, and shaped during a lifetime.

Day-to-day life in time-space involves complex mostly unconscious interactions with the other side. You [-all] are sometimes aware of dreams, though what they are and *why* they are perplexes you, mostly. Sometimes you hear voices, or feel impulses, or experience knowings, or follow hunches, and all these are all variants of connection. Sometimes you meet people and are instantly old friends, for no reason that is apparent.

Sometimes you share flashes or extensive swatches of telepathic communication. You have an instinctive knowings, you work sleepwalking, as you sometimes put it—

All these very common internal events are examples of the way your this-side (to you) life connects with the other side that is also part of you. And of course both This Side/That Side and Upstairs/Downstairs are examples of the usual physical spatial analogy. Necessary, helpful, but only analogy, and like any analogy it brings its unexpected and sometimes unsuspected baggage. So how do we portray the connection between you in the physical and you out of the physical? We could bring in an artist if you aren't too nervous about it.

As you did that time for the TGU painting!

Yes. And you never realized that till this minute, did you? Think how much else in all of your lives depends on your accessing skills from "this" side. The purpose of this diagram is to convey that on either side of the veil between physical and non-physical, any given mind may be in connection with others *on both sides*. Simple and obvious, that is, once stated—but easily forgotten while you are thinking about these things in some other context. The diagram is the simplest possible diagram to describe the situation, three being the minimum needed to express the concept.

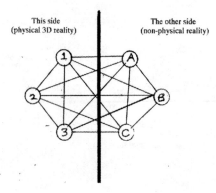

You see that, for instance, **1** (or **2**, or **3**) may connect with *only* **A** or *only* **B** or *only* **C**, or with *only* **2** or *only* **3**. A second possibility is that **1** (or **2**, or **3**) may communicate with **A** *and* **B**, or **A** *and* **C**, or **B** *and* **C**, etc.—that is, one on one side and one or more on the other). Or, **1** may similarly relate to **2** and **3** (or others, or more) and that is a third possibility—one connecting to one or more on his same side. Finally, **1** (or **2**, or **3**) may connect to one or more of **A, B, C** *and* one or more of **1, 2, 3**, etc. This seemingly more complex situation is closest to normal, little though you normally realize it. (The final set includes within it subsets that I am not bothering to describe but they should be obvious enough.)

Now given that each of the letters and numbers is in the same situation of communicating with others on both sides, you begin to get a sense of the complexity of existence and communication even at any one moment of time! And obviously it all changes moment to moment.

What we attempt to convey is so simple! So simple that when we do get the sense of it across, it is as though we haven't said anything. People's response tends to be, "well sure and so what?" In a way, that's a perfect response. In a way, it's lack of comprehension of what we are about. Just because you've heard it before doesn't mean you understood it! Just because it is a familiar sounding idea doesn't mean you are getting what is being sent.

There isn't any "there" as opposed to "here." It is *all* here (and it is all "now," but we'll get to that). There isn't any "there," anywhere! *It is all here. We* are right *here* with you. *You* are right *here* with *us*. Bob Monroe came as close as any when he defined the difference as a difference in wave-length, allowing two "things" to be in what seems to be the same space at one time without interfering with each other or even perhaps being aware of each other.

That is a metaphor, but it is close enough, and we have nothing better, so will go with it. Within that metaphor, we ask you to visualize your condition. *You* are here at a certain wave-length suitable to life in time-space (slowed down, it is usually said). *We* are here at a certain wave-length suitable to life *outside of* time-space—speeded up, so to speak. It is only an analogy, but a useful one. You can "speed up"; we can "slow down" and—communication occurs. We aren't sending to you from far away because we *aren't* far away. We are *here!* Just as *you* are *here!* There is no need for you to assume that non-physical reality is some-where "far away." *We* are *here*; *you* are *here*. If you live in Alberta, say, or Peru, or Hawaii—*we* live there. It doesn't seem so to you because we have the ability to move else-where and else-when at will, and thus one might ask what that does to the concept of residing anywhere—the answer is, *we* live where *you* live. We are separated by the vibrational difference (though—it is an anal-ogy!) between space-time and non-space-time. It is simple. We can't say it any simpler than that. But—can you hear it?

Now, a definition or two. *You* are *here* (by definition) always, and where *you* are, we are. That you cannot always experience us does not make us cease to exist. In a very real way, *we* live where *you* live. If you build paradise, we inhabit it with you. If you build hell, or by neglect build a wasteland, we are there with you. It cannot be otherwise, nor would we wish it to be. Closer to the nub of things—you, in the physical, living here-and-now, can *act*. *You* shape the physical world, and we live in the exten-sion of the world that is beyond the physical. You injure your-selves or each other and we live with the result—in fact, we experience it in more-than-physical-realism!

Does this begin to give you an idea of why physical Theater is important to us? (It doesn't matter what else you have read! While you are with us, stay with us. You can always re-think and counter-think later.) The physical is the place where one can act in a way that one cannot, outside the physical. This does not mean that the physical is the only place that is "real"; it means it is the place of delayed consequences, which has its advantages and disadvantages. It is only in physical 3D Theater that we see the phenomenon and results of delayed consequences. This does not mean that physical is the only game in town, just that it is a particular and peculiar venue.

Only One Thing Exists

Hold in mind the fact that we are proceeding from one overview: All the world (that is, all of reality) is *one* thing; there is no *absolute* division into two or more, even in the world of polarities. (This itself could be a topic for the future.) No division into kinds can be other than relative. Therefore different "levels" of physical reality will be seen to repeat the structure of other "layers"—and ultimately it will be seen that even the "layers" are merely convenient illusions, like any other "units." In a *real* way, not as metaphor at all, the microscopic and macroscopic levels interpenetrate each other. They are the same. Not merely the same substance; they are *the same*. But you probably don't yet have the background to even intuit the correctness of this statement, let alone understand it. Let's say only this, for the moment, and then go on to other things with you bearing in mind that this is the perception we proceed from: *Size is merely a physical manifestation*, and is irrelevant in its non-physical manifestation.

You're right, I can't quite grasp it, although that last sentence seems to strike a distant chord.

The entire experiencing of a physical world is an elaborate and instructive metaphor, but it is not the ultimately real experience that it appears to be.

So. Three levels of mind as seen from any level. We "guys upstairs" experience you, Frank, as a strand, and we are a strand to that above us. You, Frank, experience strands, which experience you as the group-mind of which they each function as a strand-mind. And so up and down the scale without limit, for there is no ultimate up or down because it is not actually the smaller-to-larger polarity it appears.

I had an altered-state experience in the black box once, I vaguely remember, in which I perceived that as I looked into smaller and smaller, it got larger than me somehow.

You are not remembering it right. Your physical brain tries to reinterpret experience to "make sense" of it, as it does everything in life. It isn't that the smaller *gets* larger but that it *is* larger, as well. But we cannot stay to discuss this. Too long and still insufficient background conveyed. It is enough that you somewhat remember what you experienced, even if you could not make sense of the experience.

So—from any point of view, three levels of mind. That being the case, we need only examine the composition of the nearest, to shed light on the others—both the two directly perceived and any others, either perceived in extraordinary circumstances or never perceived or perceivable at all. That's one task—examine the nearest as it functions *in itself.*

Then, examine the three layers as they function *in relation.* How does group-mind express in the life and functioning of a person-mind, and how does a strand-mind, and how does the group-mind function in relation to either and both? Don't be overwhelmed by the size and scope of the conception. It is actually easiest this way, for it will continually tie together experience and concepts previously seeming unrelated.

You must, you see, overcome the continual and often unsuspected effect of the spatial analogy if you are to grasp the actual nature of the interaction of "levels." A group-mind is not larger than a person-mind; a strand-mind is not smaller than either. Size does not validly enter in it. Mind is not physical and does not exist within physical restriction.

But your brain is wired by its entire experience of earth—of 3D—to correlate things by size. To learn to think in other ways, it requires some framework to array those things on. A theoretical physicist uses mathematics. As long as he remains within that framework he can think thoughts and envision relationships that *vanish* (or at any rate are without application) as soon as he returns to everyday life. This, not because his mathematical model is cloud-cuckoo-land, but because outside his alternative framework he finds himself unable to sustain the intellectual model he well understands within it. Neither mathematics nor science is your "thing." Others will be able to translate those frameworks. Your gift and your preference and your affinity (three ways to say the same thing) is to speak plainly so that you de-mystify. So—the alternative framework you employ cannot be mathematics.

No, nor would it serve those who are listening to this.

That's what we just said. And neither will theology work even if you knew enough or learned enough to employ it.

No, because they would be unable and unwilling to follow it for emotional and historical and cultural reasons, and for ideological and political reasons.

So you return to your roots. Not history, exactly, but biography. And autobiography.

Spiritual Influences on the Consciousness

The Catholic dogma you were given as a child said the purpose of life was "to know love and serve God in this world and be with him in the next." Your catechism spoke truly, but it spoke to an earlier age and a different way of being, and was dead to most ears by the time it was taught to you more than half a century ago. How much deader, then, in 2010! And yet eternal truths are not dependent upon the fashions of any one time; they merely need to be dressed up. If they do not resonate when seen with new eyes, how true can they be?

To know, love, and serve God in this world. If you're thinking of "God" as a remote judgmental being who is going to judge you when you're finished and maybe send you to hell, that's going to be an important thing when you are a child—and it's going to fall away from you when you cease to be a child, because nothing in your life will lend it credibility. It won't make any sense in the terms it was presented in. (Besides, you should love something that might send you to hell?)

Now, note, the fact that such childish concepts fall away from people as they cease to be children does not mean that they disappear. *It means they fall into the unconscious*, where they continue to operate, unsuspected, as programming for various robots. Many a person is vehement against religion (rather than indifferent, or ambivalent, or supportive, or quietly dismissive) because he or she is actively fighting remnants of such discarded or forgotten beliefs. The vehemence comes because they are at war with themselves.

But to return. In examining anything, look to find what is really being said, by trying *with as much intellectual sympathy* (even if tentative and provisional) *as you can bring to bear*. In the absence of intellectual sympathy—that is, of a willingness to approach the subject humbly rather than from a position of already knowing—nothing can be learned. All you'll get will be polemics that will—big surprise!—reinforce the position you bring to it. You can conclusively prove that you were right, whatever your position on anything. It's merely a matter of refusing to examine with real openness and curiosity, and instead defending the established position of various strand-minds, usually only vaguely perceived by you the ringmaster.

So, look at that catechism phrase. Tell your Protestant or your materialist or your Renaissance or your scientific or your secular strand-minds to shut up for long enough for you to really examine what is being said. Reassure them that such examination won't result in your having to become a Catholic, and won't result in your having to believe in a bearded God on a cloud. *Some people will find this very difficult to do*—which should demonstrate that it is worthwhile. Others may not find it hard, but may find it not very interesting. This may show them some robots, or strand-minds, protecting their terrain by a veneer of boredom. And some may find it easy because no one inside is threatened by the act of sympathetic examination.

Whichever is your case (and it may vary by time of day or, more precisely, by which strand-minds are occupying center stage at the moment), look at it and see that, whatever the phrase meant to the devisers of the catechism, it is a paraphrase of what we have been saying. At least, it may be seen that way if we make certain assumptions.

"To know, love and serve God in this world." That is, "to experience, join with, and unite your will with your experience of a non-physical reality in which you somehow take part."

"And be with Him in the next." Or, "to be an active functioning part of that non-physical reality once you drop the body."

Isn't that a fair paraphrase of what we've been spelling out? Again, that doesn't necessarily mean that's what the catechism-makers meant. But it does mean, or let's say it hints, that the two descriptions are two different intellectual schemes for apprehending the same reality. The difference—*one* difference— is that the old religious phrasing and understanding is largely dead to the people living and those that are on their way in the Western world, which is a huge strand-mind of the world-mind. Yet it resonates and reverberates in what is still called the Third World, because the clothing fits them better. They haven't yet had five generations immersed in technology to separate them from non-physical realities.

So are we teaching theology here? Are we advocating the study of theology? Not exactly. We are saying, you may not want to reinvent the concept of the wheel even if you have to (*especially* if you have to) refashion the wheel to new uses.

I wonder if anybody is still listening. I can imagine howls of outrage, or anyway derisive smiles, at the concept of taking a catechism question and answer and considering it seriously. Everybody's caged animals will be pacing restlessly.

The question to which that was the answer is, "what is the purpose of life?" Or, as people put it, "why are we here?" If you already know, you don't need to look. But if you don't know and you *know* you don't know, it doesn't make sense to close off certain doors that have labels on them specifically promising to lead where you want to go, merely because you don't like the lettering on the door.

New Understandings

[And so one day, the casual use of an expression—not necessarily my idea, really—led to the following productive exchange.]

Gentlemen, at your service. Who's up? Pray bring whomever I need.

The word "pray" attracted me, brother. *[This is Bertram, a Norman monk who was at Salisbury, England, then Canterbury, sometime in the 1100s as best I can tell. By 2006, an old acquaintance.]* And this, by the way, is why you should watch the words you use—one reason that words are so powerful is that they vibrate particular strings, to use our "rings and threads" analogy, and so an unintended resonance may bring to light something you would rather not rouse. I do not mean this as any threat or fear-rousing picture. In my day these things were better understood than in yours, but our language describing them has become strange to you, and so for the moment our knowledge has been lost to you.

Say more, brother. And welcome. I can't quite remember but it seems to me this communication may be a first between us.

A first occurrence in this format, yes. We have exchanged words before—and you and I share many a thread and already in your life you have consciously shared a task with me and both of us with Joseph the Egyptian.

Yes, and it occurs to me you must have enjoyed my time on [the island of] Iona [in 2003].

I did indeed. Brother Columba was many hundred years in my past, you know, so in that sense it was a pilgrimage for me as for you.

Although presumably you are in contact with him on your side.

I will leave these discussions for others to have with you, but for this: Remember that you in the physical are focus-points for "the rest of you" who are not in physical. Thus, what you do affects our reality as it affects yours. Columba is a very great presence but he is activated in me—a poor way to put it, but the best I can find at short notice—by your attention on him while still being on me merely because you are flesh.

You understand? Your life, your consciousness, is automatically a focus for all your "family" of souls that are not in the physical world. What you do in your succeeding "present" moments reverberates through all of us, activating this and that thread in ways you have no ability to conceive of—and, as each of those activated threads momentarily connect rings that otherwise are not connected in activated consciousness (I know not how else to say it) your actions produce layer upon layer of unexpected and unpredictable consequences. It is lovely and is why no one is bored in the afterlife—as you call it—unless by a deliberate determination to *be* bored!

It is, of course, not merely words that set off these chains of reactions. You see the snow, you get your feet wet, you remember a dream, you quarrel, you hold a pen to paper, you read your email, you pet a dog, you change a tire—everything you do, sensory, intuitive, thinking, feeling—it all feeds back here and has its effect. In my day these understandings were couched in theological terms, and were as little understood by the mass as they are "now" in your times. This cannot be helped for two reasons:

(1) The understanding depends upon the recipient having had the experience! It is relatively easy to explain the meaning of something experienced, relatively difficult to describe the nature and meaning of something *not* yet experienced. What is religion, at its best, but a way of guiding people to have the experience, and then a framework for them to understand and benefit from that experience? In your day both functions of religion have been lost—or rather, let us say they "now" cut against the organizational experience of the religion, and so are not encouraged and frequently are actively discouraged.

(2) Not having had the experience and therefore not knowing the worth of it even if they believe abstractly that it can be real, most people are not interested enough to inquire. And so the dead bury their dead, and there is nothing to be done save to leave them to it until such time as they waken.

Bertram, it seems to me that my age needs new wineskins for new wine—except, how can the wine be described as new?

That which is new to you is new. The social format, the intellectual framework, the pattern of emotional response, will all be new, so yes it is new wine to you—even if it is the eternal unchanging water of life.

As you know, I feel that I am among the few pioneers who have been given access to Monroe's doorway. We go through the doorway; we see firsthand, and we glimpse far more, and it seems to me that from this new technological short-cut and simplified both-worlds-view can come a great supply of people who have had the experience and should then be hungry for meaning and context and a way onward—most specifically including me! And it seems, further, that we share an aversion to people telling us (as opposed to helping us to find) "the way things are." So anything we may build from this skeleton framework would need to incorporate "see for yourself first" into its framework.

To be sure. Your age is not *and cannot be* the age of faith. Neither is it, quite, any more the age of science in the sense of a knowing detached from the known. You must participate in what you study, you have no other living way open to you.

You often say you see the Monroe experience transforming into a belief system. Perhaps that is not so bad a thing, provided that one of those beliefs is: "But you must see for yourself first." Blind faith no longer serves; nor does blind skepticism, which is really blind faith-anti, or perhaps blind faith-in-the-opposite, or blind negation-faith may be a better way to express it. In your day you must see for yourselves, and more power to you. *But that does not make my age wrong* in its faith, for our circumstances were different, and our possibilities greater in some directions and lesser in others. As must be, always, everywhere. So go your way rejoicing, thanking God not only for your own time but for all times; not only for those whose faith and values are close to yours, but those who embody the polarity, for these have their legitimate place no less. No more, but no less.

As we build a habit of tolerance, other parts of ourselves are more free to emerge?

Let us say more welcome, for they are free always. Remember

your friend who forgave himself and found that in effect he forgave others within him, who then came blinking into the light.

My friend, I well remember the black-box session when I realized that you and Joseph the Egyptian and I were in our different ways, in our different times, holding the note.

Anchoring, yes. It is good work, done merely by being what we are and *intending* certain traits while refusing others. It is good work open to all, of little-suspected power, done so to speak in the darkness. What the world cannot see it does not mock, nor think to fear.

I am, these days, well aware of the assistance you and the others in my "family" provide on a day-by-day basis. The word "conscience" doesn't cover it, nor quite does "guidance." But it is a very real course-correction system that needs only to be heeded.

Heeded, or disregarded. You know Carl Jung carved on the stone "called or not called, God will be here." In a sense that is the same thing.

Three Eras, Three Views of Reality

[Apparently anyone connecting to my mind shares what I know, including connections to others on the other side. In effect, we create a shared mental space among people who may have lived far from each other in time and space. In the conversation that follows, I knew clearly which of the two personalities was speaking at any time. To make it clear here, I add J for Joseph the Egyptian and B for Bertram.]

My friends, if I can set up a three-way link here, can we get Joseph the Egyptian on the line, and Bertram?

J: You can have more or less whatever you want to have. The limiting factor always has been and always will be your own ability to receive.

Yes, I understand that now. Bertram?

B: I am here as well. There is no limit to the congregation you can have, none save practical limitations of time and consciousness.

I didn't call us together out of a whim, or only to see if it could be done. I'm wondering—years ago (in my time, of course) I experienced the three of us as holding a note, so to speak. As was pointed out, this was more by what we are *than by what we* do. *Can you both say some more about that?*

J: I shall begin, then. We three express very different understandings of the world. By "express" I do not mean what we utter, I mean we *are* expressions of our times. There were no Christians when I lived, and there are precious few, Frank, when you live, who accord with Bertram as an expression of the worlds. (Worlds, not world, because of course we all express the totality of our being—consciously or not—and part of our being is in flesh and the larger part is not, and never could be.)

Yet although we as expressions are vastly different, *what* we express is the same. White light shining through a red or green or yellow filter *expresses* differently, but expresses, as best it is able, the same white light. Surely this is obvious. Nor is it a tragedy or even a misfortune that the filters are by nature unable to express white light. This *filtering* is what they are designed to do! How else would you experience blueness or greenness if not for filters that separated out for you everything that was *not* a particular color? And is that not valuable? Is there some advantage to seeing pure white light always and only? No, the misfortune would be one forgetting or disbelieving in the existence of white light because one never saw behind the filters, and never combined the results of various filters in such a way as to deduce the source.

B: Yes, we say that man is made in the image of God, and what is this but to say that everyone is a reflection of an aspect of God? In our day we could not employ scientific analogies, nor express truth in the language of a psychology that was centuries in the future. We could express the same truths in terms that seem simple-minded and crude in your time, Frank, and would have seemed frightfully ignorant to Joseph's time. Yet the appropriate container conveyed the appropriate refreshment—or, the wineskin suited the wine.

And so the commonality is what we three are doing, is—?

B: It might be expressed in different ways. We would say obedience to the will of God, by which we mean that what you call Downstairs-you recognize your place in the scheme of things and do not inappropriately insist on pre-eminence. In matters of the human will, yes, we are on earth to choose, and hopefully to choose to do God's will even when our human nature would have us do otherwise. That is, in terms closer to yours, to act and to be and become in such a way as to advance the Upstairs connection rather than to obscure or choke it. Jesus is the model of the human self perfectly according his will with the divine self, and as he aligned his will, so he aligned his consciousness, and as he aligned his consciousness, so he received abilities and qualities that seemed—to his access-choked fellows—super-human. But miracles were never a part of Jesus' accomplishment, and neither was raising himself from death. The *achievement* was perfect alignment. All else followed.

J: In our time, as you noted in one of your sessions, we were more directly connected to what you call "the other side" and less so to other individuals, in a way that you would scarcely comprehend if you observed it, and would find repellent. Ours and Bertram's may be regarded as opposite ends of a polarity, with your age coming into a middle position. We were much of the other world and little of the physical, hence our relative disregard of social arrangements relative to the individual: We *knew* that we were each in the right place, for how else could it be? Bertram's society was much of the physical world and but little of the other world, regardless how they thought of it—that is, regardless what they *believed*, they *experienced* far less. And yours is moving through loss of faith, slowly into personal direct knowledge which will of course change everything because it will change the *base* of everything.

It seems to me that Bertram's time was closer to the other side in some ways than we are.

B: Those of us who had seen beyond the veil would argue the opposite. What is common knowledge among you could not even be heard by any save a very few. What confuses your thought is that in my day people were *emotionally* closer. They were simpler. They did not need and could not have accommodated complicated intellectual formulations. Their access came through the emotions and the senses. *This*, you see, was the function of the great Gothic cathedrals! They functioned as emotional doorways into greater connection, experienced only perhaps as an inrush of emotion, but none the less facilitating connection between man and God, or as you would say between Downstairs and Upstairs, or human and divine, or physical and non-physical. Our belief system was well worked out, and the bulk of it was argument among scholars: I tell you that the common minds of our time—and that includes kings, it is not a class distinction but an intellectual one—knew only the basics of a story, but that story gave them hope and meaning and—the important thing—gave them their only real hope in our time of access. It is because your time does not understand this that you are being asked to pass on the word. Later ages became capable of more, and then demanded more, and society then changed in response. But although the pious of those ages may have despaired at this new lack of faith, all was well; turbulence often merely foretells the coming of a new age—a new arrangement of beliefs and values and strivings. Do not expect to recognize in advance what has not yet manifested; merely, remain open to an understanding that may come or may not, and in any case will come only in its own time, in its own way, according to the laws of its being.

J: You are moving to a new place on the polarity, closer to your fellows than we were, closer to direct access to the other side than Bertram's times were. Your experiences will not repeat either, but will be one more filter through which to see the world, which will in turn limit and so focus the filters that are individuals in those times.

Souls, Traits, and Reincarnation

[Another time, I talked to Joseph Smallwood (though I may not have his name right), who I think of as a "past life" that is part of me.]

Joseph, my friend, how do you spend your time? (Don't think I don't know this is a planted question, coming out of the blue "because" I just looked back at an entry here, but still I'd like to know.)

I assume that you know that in talking to Joseph you are talking to the completed soul—that is what it looks like to you, anyway. Let me tell you the difference life on earth makes, and you will gradually get the idea. You go to earth one thing and you come out something pretty different! That's the whole point of it. You're used to talking about bundles and threads and all that, and that is well and good from TGU's side—that's the big picture, the overview, you know. But that's more like *theory* than the way it seems to us doing it.

I don't remember ever not existing, any more than you do. Seems to me I've always been here, only I came out of a fog, sort of. I don't mean that's how I feel since coming over, I mean that's how it felt when I was in a body. You know how it is, you're in a body. Wherever you are, you're in a chain of memories, and those memories extend backwards but after a while they sort of peter out and it's all mist and fog.

First we find ourselves in a body, and it takes a while to learn to use the thing, pulling and hauling till we figure it out. That's physically. Then when we go through puberty there's another whole set of gears to learn, emotional ones this time, and at the end of it we ain't kids any more, but men, or women. Well, I say "emotional" but you'd probably say chemical and such; don't matter as long as we're talking about the same thing.

Well, as you know very well, we go along day by day following our inclinations you might say, or trying to if the world will let us, and as we live we shift ground, mostly without much noticing, and the person at 30 ain't at all the same as he was at 20 or will be at 40. I mean, he *is*—things continue—but he's different, too. All that living, all that choosing, means he's down various paths, and finally, long or short, the path is over and he's over here.

Now—remember, I'm telling this the way we mostly experience it, not the way it could be seen from a wider perspective—for all extents and purposes each new person that gets born has been created new for the occasion. The psychic materials that went into him—all the threads that the guys talk about—they are like raw material, like the chemicals and all that made the baby's body. As far as you yourself are concerned, every thing in you is raw material that went into making you. It's what was *used*, but it wasn't *you*.

You understand what I'm doing here? I'm trying to say that each lifetime is a creation more than it is a continuity. I'm saying

Joe Smallwood may be the result of other lives on the spiritual side the way he is on the physical side, but in neither case are his ancestors *him*! Until Joe Smallwood was born, there *wasn't* any Joe Smallwood, from the beginning of time, no matter how many people's lives went into the making of him. But once he was born and lived, he's going to live forever. There's your "infinite stick with one end" that Voltaire made fun of, but it don't matter what he thought, true's true.

So, now. One way or another, old Joe Indian *[his nickname among the whites]* dies. That's it for him in the physical. It ought to be obvious enough. Once in, once out. *Joe*, as a person, as a separate being, is *finished* with the physical! He can't come back any more than 1842 can come back. Nor would we want to or need to!

I think Dr. Jung ought to explain, he can do it better.

And I take it that this was pre-arranged, not that I doubted it. Welcome, Dr. Jung.

It may assist you to conceptualize it if you keep in mind the two ways of describing a personality given in a horoscope. One is the individuality, or the essence; the other is the personality.

Personality is often seen as merely a mask, a social adaptation behind which one hides one's true nature. Yes, this often happens, but the true distinction between essence and personality is between the eternal spirit and the localization of spirit that is confined to the one lifetime. These are not the same thing. They do not have the same origin, or nature, or destiny. Confusing spirit and soul has led modern man to discredit both.

Without spirit—without the threads your analogy uses to describe all the factors making up your being while you are in a particular body—obviously there could *be* no life. How could you have a life without the million threads of traits that you express? How could you have life without the very thing that *is* life, the animating spirit?

The spirit, as father, and physical material, as mother, create a new life. That is, they anchor the potential in a single place and time, from which point it begins to make its way as a separate individual. Of course, when I say "father" and "mother" I do not want you to confuse an analytical description of function with the person who is the father and the person who is the mother.

The new life created—not just the body, which by itself is powerless to maintain itself, but the body animated by spirit— we may call a soul. Souls are always by definition rooted in one time, one place. There is only one conception, one birth, per soul, as there is only one death. Its life is shaped entirely within those bounds while in the physical—and the essence of the soul then passes to the other side entirely, when the body dies off.

Yes, I hear the objection as to the use of time as an absolute and, for the matter, the ignoring of alternate reality versions. But complex matters must be clearly understood in their essentials before it is safe to introduce and relate complexities and seeming contradictions and genuine conundrums—for life will always have mystery around it, you know.

So, you see, if you are to think of reincarnation, it is not to be found in the context of a given soul. Joseph Smallwood and Carl Jung are gone and will not be back. But *what they are* may be back as traits, as memories, as preferences—and they may be back in unexpected and surprising combination. Joe Smallwood's preference for nature mysticism with David Poynter's occult exploration and John Cotten's stubborn matter-of-fact concentration on getting through the day somehow.

Do you see? It may be instructive for you to consider yourself to split into water and ice cubes after you die. The ice cubes are solid, definite, structured; that is Joseph's soul, the structure he shaped in his years of life. The water is *the same thing*, entirely—but fluid, formless, without boundaries, and this is the spirit that flowed through Joseph's life, or you may say the traits, the threads, that went into the making of him, and were lived as him and shaped by his decisions and experiences.

And the water goes into new mixtures, yet the ice cube remains to be talked to—for instance—by people doing this.

That's correct.

[After taking a break, I returned to the subject.]

So, Joseph, my friend, how do you spend your time?

There wasn't any way you could understand my answer if we hadn't gone through the material we just gave you.

I know, I'm just razzing you.

Oh, I know it. But I'm just saying. Well, you see, if you have got the picture that you're talking to a soul, not a spirit, and therefore I ain't going to be reincarnating from this form—in other words, that I'm here now and I'm a finished product as far as the earth is concerned, then we can talk. But understand, *in a different sense,* everything that went into being Joe Smallwood *and came out of being* Joe Smallwood is available and might go into the making of anybody, you included. It's just, you're talking to the ice cube, not the water. You want to know how I spend the time, which, I take it to mean you want to know what happens to the soul after death.

Yes. Maybe I should give some history here. I instinctively believed in reincarnation since I first heard of it, as a boy. I believed in it more after my experiences starting in 1987 and especially 1992. But over time I have come to think that the conventional explanation is too simple and it doesn't explain things I have experienced and heard second-hand about people in the afterlife. The guys gave us an intensive tuition into the way things are, starting in August, 2001—yet at the same time, sessions in the black box the year before, and three years after, seemed to add complications. So I'm just trying

to understand it all. I think we're at the edge of really coming up with
a scheme that will explain things usually left hanging.

Yes. The first thing is that people in your day—and in mine too, come to think of it—keep the two worlds too far apart. They act as if the spirit world, or the world of souls, hasn't got anything to do with the physical world, and so they don't have very good ideas about any of it.

There's the spirit world, and the soul's world, and the physical world, and they all are part of the same thing, and there ain't any use pretending they're separate rather than interrelated. Now in Monroe terminology, you'd say Focus 27 for the spirit world, and belief-system territories (focus 24, 25 and 26) for the soul's world. Can you see that this mixes up two things that oughtn't to be mixed up? Well, maybe that ain't quite fair, and maybe it ain't a fair description of the Monroe world. I suppose you might say that Focus 27 is part of the soul's world, except it—

There's a big difference between Focus 27—that looks to the possibility of reincarnation for one thing—and the belief system territories that are concerned with where the souls go who have some definite ideas of the afterlife (though that ain't quite it) or Focus 23 for them that don't, or are for some reason unable or unwilling to fit into the accepted places.

So, to envision a soul going to Focus 27 and reincarnating is to mix up the definition in the middle of the sentence. No, I can tell you what's going on. When you retrieve somebody from Focus 23, or from one of the belief-system territories, you free them from single vision, and it's like you free the water from the ice cube. The ice cube remains, and it can stay where it is, or move somewhere else, but it's still an ice cube. It isn't going to reincarnate no matter how you force it; that's what's going to happen to the water, if anything. But you can sense the freeing of the ice cube to flow, which will seem to you like it's reincarnating.

Is that at all clear to you? John Cotten's Clara, who became Mrs. Emerson, who became the woman in your Gateway (naming no names) was, as you later realized, stuck all that time, stuck from the 1770s until 1997. Yet she "became" two other people that you know of, and more besides probably. How could that be? The answer is, the *ice cube* didn't do anything or go anywhere. The ice cube went on being stuck until it was waked up. But what happened to the *ice cube* hadn't a thing to do with what happened to the *water*. It was the water that "became" the others; and like I say, it didn't become those other people just as it had been, but mingled and added and subtracted with other parts of other people.

Of course, all these distinctions are wrong but what are you going to do when you've got to use language to get *anything* across?

So, Joseph, my friend, how do you spend your time?

I'm getting to it. There's lots more playgrounds than earth, you know. Earth has the advantage that it gives us solidity; it gives us as you might say the habit of sustained focus. Anybody who has been in a physical life has been hardened, sort of. They've been given an experience that shapes them more definitely than them that haven't. I can't offhand think of a better way to put it. I'm more *me*, more self-conscious, more firm in my ideas you might say, than I would be if I hadn't had a physical life. So now I am a resource to my friends more so than if I were simpler.

How to put it? Remember how you have been told that on this side we've all got a vibration level, and we can't move very well or very much or very far? So if one has a level of 50 and another one of 70, they've got to go through a bunch of intermediaries? But being in the earth, in the physical, is like tying together a bundle of different frequencies and they stay tied. So I can directly relate to 70, and 50, and 35, and 115, you see. That's what I mean by being more shaped.

That's how I spend my time.

That's how you spend your time—doing what?

Relating.

Sorry, but that doesn't begin to explain things.

Best I can do. You might want to talk to someone else. I am a being that's more complicated than it might have been if I hadn't been on earth; I can react to things out of my own complication and my own built-in bias. I'm a window on a certain way of seeing things. You see?

No. I'm sorry, but I just don't. It doesn't give me even a vague sense of what living on the other side is like.

That's because you're making it too hard. And, this new format, going right into the computer instead of slower by pen, don't help. It might take a little time. That's enough for now.

Well, all right. I do appreciate the effort. It leaves me with only one question.

Yeah, I know. How do I spend my time?

Correct.

Don't forget that you got *prompted* to ask that question.

That's right, so I did. Hmm.

[If that exchange left you a bit perplexed, you aren't the only one. Yet it provided ideas to chew on, as so often happens in these conversations. Although the guys have made a lot of things clearer to me, I can't say that they have ever given me a clear idea of life on the non-physical side—at least, not yet!]

Significantly Different Lives

The underlying idea behind reincarnation is that a unit removes from a lifetime, and if in the proper condition doesn't have to return to the world of illusion, but if tempted back, returns and again takes on a lifetime. (This is of course only a rough approximation of a complex and intellectually developed system of thought and perception.)

We propose to you that it is the identification of the unit that has led to conceptual problems—and that resulted *from* conceptual problems in the first place! With the proper re-conceptualization of the unit involved in reincarnation schemes, we can sign off on them. (And if you don't see the pitfall implied and contained in the very mention of a conceptualization, well—you should. To make a distinction is to make an error. It's just that it cannot be helped, either by Buddhists or by we guys upstairs.)

What is the purpose of life, really? To cure one's ignorance? To overcome one's one-sided-ness or one's faults? To have an interesting time for its own sake? To add to the store of interesting movies available on the other side ("The Life Of Frank, or, the amazing non-adventures of an intuitive" or any other way you could dramatize your life and see it one way)?

We offer you a different concept of the purpose of life—not as an either/or but as at least an equally important adjunct to the others that have been proposed over the years. As with everything else, there is no *one* way to see it. One aspect of the theory of relativity we entirely agree with is that there is no one place to judge from; therefore all judgments are as much an expression of perspective as of measurement. That said, we will insist that the conventional explanations of life do not express the relationship and function that we are emphasizing, and therefore they miss the very important purpose life serves and can serve more consciously. Everything we say comes from one central idea:

Your life has meaning regardless, but can have greater

meaning if you consciously cooperate with its underlying purpose, for thus your experience is richer and deeper and your effective horizons much broader.

A person comes into being. For the moment forget just *how* it comes into being (that is, the question of who and what is choosing among the potential physical elements that will express or will, rather, have the possibility of expressing). By whatever methods and through whatever agents, a person constellates from the parents' combined potential pool of traits, and thus the new person is limited—given shape—in time and space and physical heredity.

Why those parents and not different ones? Why that time and place rather than others in which those same parents might have conceived? Questions of who choose and why did they choose this rather than that are always inherent. Some see it as a council of advisors who help the soul-between-lives to "plan" a life. Others see it as a form of external judgment with which the soul-between-lives concurs, in one way or another. Can you see that the question of who (or what) is being formed and by what rules of its nature (or rules of some other kind) it is shaped, is not addressed, but begged?

If you see each life as in fact not unitary but community-natured—as we do—then it is easier to see that each new lifetime is *significantly* different in composition. Different heredity, different circumstances. What is the continuity within that group, among those lives? The *continuity* is what we are seeking here—the spiritual heredity. The continuing aspect of spirit that some call a traveling soul. We prefer to use soul to refer to each specific person-group, yet spirit is not divisible. Can you see that there is a *gap* in the concepts?

A soul is a given person-group's common factor, common expression of its nature.

A spirit is the non-physical continuation that comes into a person-group from somewhere and remains (or goes elsewhere, depending on how you choose to see it) after the person-group is no longer in the body.

Where is the personal aspect of undivided spirit that experiences itself in various person-groups? Spirit is indivisible, yet it has aspects that manifest as separate—how shall we think of these aspects, in connection to various person-groups *and* in connection to itself regardless of person-groups?

Any memory presupposes something to *contain* the memory. How could one retain memories of a past-life trauma if there were no common factor between present-life and past-life beings? And clearly the common factor can't be physical heredity, because if it were, one could only incarnate within one's own line of ancestry. And while that theme bears thought as an example of a vision of separations and re-weavings, it isn't the case in fact.

A Matter of Definition

You're saying, I think, that the person-mind emerges during our life, and that it has a central identity (the ego? Is that what you mean?) that mistakes itself as being one thing when in fact it is a moderator of the many things, many unsuspected, that actually comprise the person's consciousness.

Yes, that's what we said. It is in this sense that each incarnation represents the birth of a new soul, for no two-person-groups can be the same, any more than any two physical genetic-and-time-and-space signatures can be the same. Not only does each soul—each mind—begin differently, it makes different choices as it goes along, and so necessarily shapes itself and becomes, so to speak, continuously more unique. But suppose two person-groups with substantially similar composition. You might think that similar forces in similar environments would produce similar choices, and similar results. Maybe, maybe not, for it truly is a matter of *choice*, not of destiny. And what each individual does with the cards he or she has been dealt is what it is all about.

So what of the sense of continuity we feel, that feels like past lives?

In a real sense, they *are* past lives, but it doesn't mean quite what you have been told it means, because the facts have always been interpreted as applying to individuals in a way that can't be accurate because the understanding of the nature of the individual isn't accurate. If a clairvoyant were to look into your aura and read your past lives, what would actually be being read? *Results!*

You mean, I think, that the end-result of a given life produced (or is?) the thing that is one of our strands.

Good. We will spell it out a little. Your person-mind contains many strand-minds, of differing complexity and nature, just as external nature has rocks, plants, animals, spirits etc. (Yes, spirits are part of nature.) That is, everything that exists comprises elements of varying complexity. Again, remember, *it's all one thing* ultimately. There are no ultimate divisions in nature. Well, one such strand-mind may be the person-mind that emerged from a life. It is the result of the choices that person-group made in its life. You see? The *results* of one life enter into another life as part of a new mixture. And everyone contains so many strand-minds as part of their person-mind—if they were all active and clamoring for attention you would be bewildered, and indeed this is some people's situation. Or, at the other extreme, if you were unaware that your consciousness is actually a moderation of competing forces, you might think yourself a unity while actually being at the mercy of every "mood"—and this also is many a person-mind's situation.

Regardless the awareness of it by the person-mind, the existence of these strand-minds is the equivalent of the existence of past lives within you, for what exactly is the difference between what we are saying here and what so many people believe, except the concept of the individual? If you see the individual as a migrating soul, that's one thing. If you see the individual as a person-group including previous person-groups, that's somewhat different. In either case the existence of memories, traits, associates, affinities etc. is the same.

I can hear someone asking, then what is the point of existence, if it isn't self-improvement, self-development?

As in evolution?

Sure. That's the big metaphor in our time.

Within the concept of evolution or outside of it, the question remains: *what* are we talking about? *[I.e., what is a person?]* After all, evolution wouldn't necessarily have anything to do with individuals. A person-group serving as strand-mind to another person-group could be quite as easily fitted into the scheme. It would still feel like growth and striving to the person-mind; it would still contribute to complexity in the group-mind (from its standpoint) to which it contributed.

But if the individual isn't a unit reincarnating, how can it evolve? And if evolution isn't the point, or isn't real, what is the point?

You and everybody who reads this *knows* what the point of existence is, you just may not know it intellectually. That is, your *life* knows; your *concepts* may not. Life is about living, and if you can provide a more all-inclusive definition of life purpose than that, we'd like to hear it. Each person-group's definition of life is going to be different, appropriately to that group. One man's meat is another man's poison. One person's absorption is another person's boredom. *But each one knows*; it's just that the ringmaster may not know, or may be so distracted by other people's definitions that he forgets or discards what he knows.

You want to know what your life is about? Look at your life! You want to know what you "should" do with your life? Look what you *are* doing! It's almost too simple to be said. We are not getting into your arguments about evolution because (a) who would it convince and (b) how would it aid *anybody*? But we will say this, merely. *Theory*, and *knowledge*, have nothing to do with your life except perhaps to orient or confuse you. All this theory we are giving you is merely to try to counterbalance some of your mental environment's voice. The thing that matters is not your theory about why you're living, but—living. That is, living out what you are. And what choice do you think you have? Are you going to live someone else's life? No, your person-group is *what*ever it is, *where*ver it is, *when*ever it is. Your task is to *live*. Obviously, living anyone else's idea of life is not what you're here for (except in so far as what someone says or does resonates within you; influence is not the same thing as advice).

To return to where we began. The ringmaster finds itself moderating a congeries of forces—of strand-minds. He does what he can. In so doing, the life of that person-mind emerges. The question of contention among these strand-minds is a worthy subject that has many aspects to be explored.

I had lay down and for some reason—you, I suppose—I thought of the past-life memories of James Leininger, who as a boy was haunted by memories that turned out to be of James Huston, a fighter pilot on that ship. Suddenly I saw it: The strand-mind within James Leininger was the person-mind of James Houston. The person-mind of James Houston had moved on to become part of a group-mind that was the person-mind of a little boy. Conceptually it is very simple!

Well, not quite so simple, but that is an accurate perception and understanding. Thus, you see, reincarnation *is* correct, for a soul moved on to live again. But reincarnation is *not* correct, because the soul did not move on to be ringmaster again, but only to be one factor of many.

Yes, and when young James moves on, James Houston will be a strand of a strand.

Not quite that simple either, but you're getting the sense of it now. And perhaps you see why we have been saying, do your work on yourself *now*, meaning while you are ringmaster, for you won't find it so easy thereafter, and may in fact find it impossible unless you receive assistance.

Not every person-group is included in a new person-group.

No, and those who are, are chosen by no rules that we know how to enumerate. You can *feel*, now, how many, many things cannot be explained while you are firmly enmeshed in wrong concepts.

A non-physical habit-pattern—a mind—newly relieved of its affiliation with the body, exists and has its awareness automatically expanded as it realizes and explores its huge number of interconnections with strands and groups. That's more than enough, for some, and they have no wish to return to become a strand in another person-mind. Others, either for specific tasks to be accomplished or from their own intrinsic interest, return to earth in a new affiliation. Well, how is the former person-mind to be a new person-mind? That person-mind forms as the sum of its strand-minds. Can someone be a strand and a ringmaster in the same person-mind? (Actually, it can seem that way, but only for a while, and even then the answer is, "no, they can't really.") So—looking at life from the viewpoint of any given person-mind, you're only new once. You only get one bite of the ringmaster apple. You don't step into the same river of life twice. But that is *not* the same as saying that you only live once and then you're never alive on earth again. Rather, it means that the particular ring that is you can only be forged once. Once created, you can play many parts in life physical and life non-physical, but you can't create yourself again, and can't be created anew again. That's just common sense. But it has a lot of ramifications for those who can ponder it in light of psychology or theology or metaphysical systems. It will throw a peculiar and intense light on many things.

Some ex-ringmasters, let's call them, will be of particular use to the purpose behind life, and they may be used as strands not once or twice but many times. Others may be of no use at all and may never serve in that capacity. (That doesn't mean they will serve no purpose or will cease to exist; it means they are not sufficiently differentiated to be useful as feedstock for new-person groups.) And, between these extremes, some ex-ringmasters will be employed as strands in some but not many new person-groups.

A couple of things to note.

1) It is not a case of an ex-ringmaster getting only one new assignment. They could get many; the only rules about it (as far as we know) concern usefulness.

2) Just because an ex-ringmaster is used in one person-group doesn't exactly mean it will or won't have further influence when that person-group in turn becomes a strand in a new group-mind. It depends on how prominent it is in the person-mind of which it forms a strand.

3) A person-group may crystallize or not. If it does, in effect a new being has been created, closer to being a unit than before because the relations of its constituent parts are relatively fixed.

4) However, this isn't really so, either, except from a certain point of view, because a strand-mind within a person-mind may play one role, have one relative importance, but play an entirely new role, of greater or lesser importance, when that person-mind is considered as having become part of another group-mind.

5) Finally and most confusingly of all, consider: All this is our explanation unavoidably crammed into the time-and-space

analogy, or model. All this *movement* isn't really movement, so much as relationship. Our description is somewhat as if we were trying to describe an abstract painting by saying the colors swirl, or this color blends into that and proceeds to that. The *movement* is analogy more than it is description, but that's part of the inherent problem of translating into 3-D terms.

Past-Life Memory

You had a stray thought that you almost forgot, that maybe "Joseph" was and is Story that you wrapped around your Perception, and this is why it is emotionally right and factually very much not in evidence.

Not a new thought, particularly.

New in that our recent discussion of the factors that go into an incarnation, showing you that the concept of reincarnation is more a matter of how you look at it than something that can be settled one way or the other—because it rests on an inadequate definition of who and what is re-incarnating, and who or what results from such an event. If in your make up are Civil-War-soldier material, and pioneer material, and Japanese monk material, and journalist material, and so much else—calling those threads "material" for convenience here—you can see now as you couldn't have seen earlier that these very real resonances would express in you in whatever their characteristic way, and you, becoming aware of them, might easily sort them into life-stories, separating them or combining them according to what seems right to you. This would be an act of fiction as much as of research, for it would be superimposing a story—Story—upon recognized traits the perception of which—Perception—was in itself accurate. Perception versus Story again, you see. The real thing, sensed or intuited, and then what your mind makes of it.

I understand the concept and it makes sense to me as a possibility—but what of people who can read other people's past lives? What of Edgar Cayce? What of James Leininger?

Again, we aren't saying that there isn't continuity between lives—we are saying that your definition—like most of the common definitions of reincarnation—rests without thinking upon the concept of individuals as units rather than as communities—person-groups, as we are calling them for convenience.

If a community is mistaken for a unit, it is natural to assume that that *unit* either reincarnates or doesn't reincarnate *as a unit.* And if it doesn't, then that's it—one life and no more. If it does then that's it—life after life after life.

And if it was never a *unit* in the first place? If there isn't any unit to move forward because the only unity was an artificial unity created by the coexistence of chosen elements within a body that served to contain them by limiting their on-going experiences to the same time and place for the duration of that body's lifetime?

Now, bear in mind—as we do—that if reincarnations have been reported in such numbers by people with no obvious ax to grind there must be a reason. That is, we should take the evidence as evidence for *something.* But the interpretation needn't be the accepted one; what is necessary is to see if the explanation takes in the salient features of the reported experiences.

In short, if what has been reported can be explained better by looking at us as communities rather than as individuals.

More or less. Yesterday we got across the fact that any new birth is going to involve a significant change in composition, if only at the physical level. This by the way is why talent may run in families (the Bach family of musicians, say). Reincarnation into the same family drastically reduces the number of new factors that the new mind has to accommodate itself to.

Now we are adding to that. Into the new container goes, not the contents of *an* old container, but perhaps parts of many, and each of these parts—strands, you have sometimes called them—brings its own unbroken but unconscious connection to its previous associations, and this goes forth forever.

That's a lot to absorb. We'll say it again differently, with slight apologies to those who got it the first time.

Each ring contains threads it shares with other containers. (A complication that we are going to ignore is that many contemporaneous containers may share a given thread. It isn't exclusive. Think how many people may have red hair, or be left-handed, at the same time on the earth.) Each thread in an incarnation amounts to a resonance with specific aspects on the other side. This is your access, and (subject to qualifications we aren't going to make here) is in fact the scope of your access. More or less, you can access what any part of you resonates to, and what that in turn connects to, and nothing more. But just remember that this is a very loose statement that will need to be qualified.

Well, if two "individuals"—two-person-groups—in the earth share the same thread, this may provide them with a source of direct connection. You may say they resonate with each other, perhaps only on that one wave-length. That isn't the same point we're making here, but try not to forget it. It's a source of what you sometimes call psychic links, or karmic ties.

Perhaps you can see that the very concept of "individuals" is useful but artificial—as we have said, a convenient fiction. When anything is so tied in with everything else in time, in space, and (outside of time-space) in various resonances to other minds that themselves are containers of various threads, where did the individual go to? It doesn't really exist. And yet of course it does exist as a functioning unit *in effect*. You each have one body, you experience your minds mostly as separate, your various component parts experience time-space at the same time, in the same place, throughout a lifetime, and hence develop a teamwork and an accustomed unity that seems to you in life to be your nature, and that serves in the afterlife as the enduring result of that life. So—you are individual *in a sense*. You are all part of all-that-exists in another sense. It's mostly in how you want to see it, how you concentrate on this aspect rather than that aspect of your existence.

We need to speak of strands and cables—your conceptions, but maybe yours more from good listening than from original thought—but we'll need you fresh, for it will take some explanation. So this is as good a place to stop as any.

Nearly 8 AM. Tempted to come back for a second bite of the apple, having sent out what we got earlier.

We can try. Cables. You have sensed that associations of traits may come to have an autonomous existence—moving as a unit, so to speak. And this provides the bridge you have been looking for between individual traits and the person-group that people call an "individual."

Although the entire discussion is repeatedly in danger of falling into the trap of misplaced concreteness of image, we proceed.

Suppose the simplest of traits. Red hair, say. Such may be considered a unit. Hair-trigger temper, another. Each to be considered an element in the chemistry analogy—neither reducible to a simpler form.

Now suppose that red-hair and a hair-trigger temperament come to be associated so often, in so many people over time, that anyone observing red hair is tempted to suspect the presence of a hair-triggered temper. That red hair/hair-trigger may be considered to have a life of its own as what you might call a secondary layer of traits, or—what?—a compound element, perhaps. Not everyone with red hair has this temper; not everyone with this temper has red hair. Therefore the combination cannot be considered primary, in a way that either can be. And yet you may say that it has a life of its own—it may be considered as a unit.

We have no intention of trying to work our way up the scale toward ever-more-complex units, but the idea should be clearer. You can see that the physical, emotional and mental traits that get passed down through physical families may be simple or complex (some are simple, some not) but even the complex ones could be analyzed into simpler parts; however, from long usage together, they function as units. That is, over time, combinations such as red hair/temper become fused so that one often presupposes the other.

Remember, though, that although each may suggest the other, that is hardly the only link that either will suggest. Red hair may for instance suggest great sensitivity. Temper may suggest high-strung life internal or external. And any of these connections is as valid as any other.

When you move up the scale somewhat, to more complex associations, you may find, for instance, "the military mind" or "the artistic disposition" or "the wastrel" or "the workaholic." Although you tend to encounter any of these in the context of a given person (and tend to consider that person a unit rather than a community), it will be instructive for you to consider them as building-blocks. That is, although a given person-group may exhibit some of these—what shall we call them?—perhaps building-blocks is as good a term as any—someone exhibiting them didn't *invent* them and doesn't have exclusive use of them, any more than anyone can patent and license left-handedness.

Well, perhaps our point becomes obvious. A person-group consists of many building-blocks, as well as they do individual traits. Those building-blocks may be regarded as strings made from many threads always in the same connection. And the next layer of association and greater combination perhaps we should call rope—made of many strings, and then cables made of many ropes. The ultimate cable might be everything (or less than everything, depending) that went into the fashioning of the life of another person-group. Or rather, it might include everything or many things that came *out of* that particular person-group.

That is to say, what the person-group did with that life will be different from what it began that life with, and presumably the result will be more useful than the preparation.

Remember: any new incarnation must by the nature of things be limited by the physical heredity of the parents. Given that this obviously extends to farthest antiquity (each generation having its inheritance from the previous ones) the potential material pool thus is vast. However, in practical terms it is not unlimited. We won't go into that now. What matters at the moment is that in the forming of any new incarnation, the properties of the cable—whatever is being brought forth—must interact with the properties of the new body, in other words its inheritance, and so there may be—*will be*—conflict. This conflict enlarges the scope of your expression of free-will in determining what you wish to become, and at the same time doesn't make your internal or external lives any easier.

Fluctuating Consciousness

Writing in a journal book is a good image for living life in 3-D. The only page you write on is the current blank page. Each written page recedes psychologically and—shall we say mentally, or emotionally, or both. The current page is of importance to the task of the moment. The previous pages might be looked at as being merely to bring you to the latest page, or might better be seen as each one forming a page in a whole, each having its own intrinsic importance; no page having been written *for the sake of* any given future page, yet each forming a link in the chain of pages. The analogy is not perfect—only an exact replica could be a perfect analogy, and what good could that do anyone?—but it will serve.

In life one has periods of intense immersion in a given experience, and then perhaps that experience is gone forever as one moves on to other things. Being the parent of a newborn, or an infant, for instance, is something radically different from life before or after the event. Being a school child, or a young married, or any of what are thought of as the stages of life, marks a leafing-off. But this is obvious. Your lives are not monotones even when monotonous. As notes must vary if a different tune is to be played, so your discontinuities are a necessary part of the continuity that is any one human life.

And I hear you saying, each such life is a discontinuity in the larger life.

That's right. And it is true on any scale you care to apply, for life—reality— is *all one thing* regardless of appearance. If you were reading a musical score and could not see the scale for what it is—a sort of reining-in of variation to produce a set effect—you might think it random; you would very likely think it a mass of separate items whether coordinated or not. And it is true that it could be looked at that way. But a higher, more comprehensive view sees that the mass of notes have what you might call a contingent existence, whose purpose embodies them all because it transcends any one of them, or any combination of them. Thus, any life, and life in general, up and down the scale of the great chain of being.

It is because your time has lost sight of the *meaning* of the score that it thinks each given note of ultimate importance, which quickly amounts to thinking any given note of no importance at all. But if you can regain the sense of the music as a whole, you will automatically value the notes comprising it at their proper value. For, is a C of greater, or lesser, value than any other note? Is one chord intrinsically valuable—and does it exist except as a combination of notes, and does it have meaning—except in a context beyond itself?

You know all this. We are veering off into the "why" of things when we intended to provide you with your own intuition of the "why" by setting out a better understanding of the "how" of things. But perhaps there is nothing lost in occasionally reminding the studio audience why we are all cooperating in this explanation.

To resume the exploration of the "how":

Consider the consciousness with which you are experiencing these words. It is provisional and temporary, and in your life serves only as a bridge between the present moment it is reading and the overall pattern that is your soul. At any given moment, your consciousness has different components, hence a different flavor, a different purpose—or purposes, for you usually have more than one at any given time.

That momentary consciousness may be looked at like an electrical field, volatile, unstable, unsubstantial, and important only for what it can transform. The electricity in your computer is not valued or even recognized for itself but for the work it makes possible. Or—another analogy—your consciousness at any moment is like the RAM in that computer, filled each moment with different content depending on what programs you have been running, what data you have been flowing through it. But if that RAM ever stops flowing, stops fluctuating, you experience it as a computer *locking up*. It cannot function as it was designed *unless* it flows, and fluctuates, hence is highly impermanent.

Remember always, your mind is non-physical; it translates into the physical (as far as you can be aware normally) through the brain. The brain has rules established partly by its architecture and partly by the firmware installed. Translation errors, or perhaps we should say biases, are inherently probable, hence they might as well be considered part of the package. To use your joke, an unfixable bug becomes a feature.

The interface between the brain and the mind is your unique makeup. And the interface between brain/mind and the passing moment is your fluctuating consciousness. That fluctuating consciousness is the means by which your life makes its impression on your mind (your soul)—and thereby on the group-mind. In other words, each moment is a moment of flux, of choice, and therefore each moment is the unique opportunity to affect your soul and the entire scheme of things. Fortunately for you as individuals, no given individual can affect the whole very much. Where would you be if anyone could? And yet no one's input is negligible, nor can you see at any moment what will be seen as important and what will not. This paradox cannot be resolved within binary logic—that is, within the mental world as it exists when filtered through the brain. You'll just have to trust the sense you get that the information resonates.

I am starting to experience the limitations of the way we are working. I begin to get too tired just as we are in full flow. I get the sense that if we could continue, we could get vastly deeper stuff.

But that is not a path open to you. Do you care to teach people by your example to burn themselves out, as Edgar Cayce did, as Jane Roberts did? And anyway there is a better way, but it involves *work* as well as *effort*. There's a difference.

I'm listening.

Yes, perhaps you finally are. All right, then. The *effort* is doing what you have been doing—basically, taking dictation. The *work* is what you must begin to do, or do more consistently. You must *think about* what has been received, and—in your case, Frank—reshape it so that it may teach others. A book that can be absorbed in a few sittings is likely to be more influential than a mass of material, however valuable, that has to be absorbed day by day as you and your guinea pig/volunteers *[reading the transmissions day by day as I transcribed and sent them on via the Internet]* are doing. In the case of those volunteers, and any who come to read these words, your *work* is to think about and *make part of you* what resonates herein. What does not resonate, leave untouched, and do not feel obliged to "correct" what has been given; merely give your own take on it, as Frank is going to give his take on it. *This is not scripture* and is not meant to be blindly accepted nor blindly attacked. It is an instruction manual translated from a foreign language, which means it has valuable instructions perhaps occasionally garbled unintentionally.

Can we return to the volatile nature of consciousness? I'm sorry I interrupted, in a way.

No harm. We are always on plan B. But the time is running out, as always.

Let us say this. If you will begin to realize—some of you already know it well, abstractly, as a concept, but if you come to *experience*, moment by moment—that your momentary consciousness is continually fluctuating, continually is made up of different elements, just as you have come to see that different "guys upstairs" enter and leave that consciousness perceived or unperceived, identified or unidentified—*then* you can begin to understand the porous nature of who you and we really are, why we say truly, without exaggeration, that the individual is a convenient fiction. This is the key to many things, this volatility of consciousness, and it is here that we shall resume.

All right. Thanks, as ever.

The Porous Nature of Consciousness

Let's devote a few words to the porous nature of your consciousness. We think we did indeed get across something of the nature of a voluntary consciousness as a halfway house among many influences, but perhaps it would be as well to remind you that the word "layer" or "level" implies a flatness and solidity and definiteness that are quite mistaken as concepts in this connection. Think instead, perhaps, of clouds. Your—our—brain might almost be looked at as one localized area of a continuing lightning storm, lighting up various areas of the overall cloud in such a way as to make the areas appear to be more distinctly divided into sections or units than is true. This analogy has its problems, but it has its instructive aspects, too, so we will pursue it for a bit—reminding you first that it is an analogy, a map, not a territory, and in fact not even a map so much as an impressionistic interpretation of a naturalistic painting of a map. In other words, as we said, an analogy.

Think of some world like Venus or Jupiter where the entire atmosphere could be looked at as one huge cloud, and forget the boundaries of that cloud-atmosphere in outer space or on the planet's surface. We want to raise an image in your minds of a huge expanse, as changeable as air, as locally organized as storms, as invisible as any atmosphere, and as stratified, those strata being only loosely and one might say temporarily defined.

No hard and fast edges.

No edges, correct. Perhaps you have a temporally persistent feature such as Jupiter's Red Spot, but even in such a feature, it persists only because the *pattern* persists while the constituent molecules of gas continually move in or out or about it.

In such a fluid but not featureless or homogenous mass, can you see that geographers are going to have a hard time drawing boundary lines? How do you set frontier guards if the frontier itself moves all about the place continuously? Yet, again, if there are no hard-edged lines, still there are zones of division that result in, or rather result from, differences in composition that are organized, persistent, and meaningful as expressions of variation in condition resulting from the underlying conditions set up by the nature of the planet whirling through space.

Again, remember our purpose here. We want to free your consciousness from ideas that restrict your ability to intuit more productive relationships.

Now, if, within this vast sea of atmosphere with its own rules of being, we concentrate on any particular bit of it, our area may have a certain cohesion for some reason, but defining it is necessarily going to be *arbitrary*. It will be a separating for the sake of clarity of things that belong together quite as much as the things that are contained within the unit you create by your definition. Can you write boundaries in sea-water? Only as abstractions. The water itself flows. We could use an ocean as an example nearly as well as an ocean of atmosphere, and either analogy would have its particular drawbacks and advantages.

You can see perhaps why we discouraged you from starting to sketch the porousness of things. To think in terms of levels is well and good, but not if it exaggerates the solidity of the level at the expense of its continuity wherever divisions are made. We still don't want the illusion of individuality sneaking back in through the side door. It is difficult to find a three-dimensional model for a non-three-dimensional reality. We are tempted to explore the tendril-and-plant analogy but that sacrifices all the fluidity of the model we need. (It might be instructive in another context, of course. Everything in life provides analogies; the trick is to discover what the analogies refer to.)

Let us discard analogy for the moment and say it straight, and perhaps the appropriate analogies will suggest themselves. What we mean to say is simple enough, it is merely unfamiliar. But sometimes the clarification (the analogy) itself requires clarifying, and hence is better set aside for the moment.

Revert to the idea of strand-mind, person-mind, and group-mind, each being similar in composition but each functioning in a specialized way relative to minds at other levels. Obscured in this model is the very important communication and interaction person-mind to person-mind, that is, communication at the same level. Given that it occurs at the level you are familiar with (the person-mind), and given that we are discussing mind, not body—in other words given that we are discussing a non-physical not a physically-dependent phenomenon—perhaps you can see that what is true at your level is also true at the group and at the strand levels. Consciousness is a matter of input from all other levels including other consciousnesses at the same level.

Now, if any given bit of consciousness includes input from other layers, and if other bits of consciousness also include input from other layers, and if the same group-mind contains strands that each consider themselves independent person-minds, and each strand-mind is itself the group-mind of strands of its own, is it not one inseparable swirl? This for the moment undervalues the *separateness* of things because concentrating on the *unity* of things; nonetheless, it is one valid aspect of reality. Everybody is connected not as neighbors with boundaries, but as a cloud or an ocean with separation more by specific gravity or buoyancy or by the pattern of established currents.

You will remember that we have long tried to explain the strands as connecting to other bits at different wave-lengths, or specific gravity, or buoyancy. This is what we were getting at. If a given person-mind comprises strands at many different levels (there's that word back again) it in effect lives in each of these layers at the same time. A Hemingway may thus occupy a huge range of positions because his person-mind's strands include such widely different levels. A highly specialized person's person-mind might by contrast comprise huge numbers of very similar strands, rendering him or her relatively blind to much larger segments of reality so as to put in higher contrast the brilliantly lighted segments it concentrates on.

You are born with a limited range of options: There is no expanding the range of strands that are alive to you. But that limited range is immense. It is your alphabet, your palette, your raw material. By your choices among the strands you decide and create. The links you strengthen are the links you carry over to this side when you drop the body. The links you never notice, or disregard (not, though, reject, which is a different thing), do not.

This is something that I believe you have not said before.

No. One concept at a time is quite enough of a job! But surely you can see that if, at death, you were the same as you were at birth, nothing would have been accomplished. You would have no gifts to bring to the higher self, so to speak, no additions to make to the group-mind. Your time on earth would have been a non-event, a nothing. This cannot happen, as life and the passage through time impels you to choose continuously, but there is a difference between the sculptor tapping bits off a rock in order to make manifest what—for the moment—only he can see, and someone hitting a rock at random. Don't live your lives at random. It's a waste of opportunity.

But are not some people doomed to live a life at random because of the initial makeup of their person-group?

No. But this is a large subject. We will begin on it but will scarcely finish.

Any given life has several coexisting purposes and processes. What is child's play for one person-group is higher mathematics for another, and is an appropriate field of study for third. Every person-group has within it, and before it, its appropriate task that may be attacked well or badly. This is one more reason not to judge one's self or that of others, because you don't begin to understand what the various purposes are or how they are to be addressed or how they may interfere with each other or reinforce each other within the given person-group.

Instead of thinking of strand-mind as simple-minded or less conscious or in any way different from person-mind, or person-mind in relation to group-mind, consider that at each level are some who are at all possible levels of complexity and field of inquiry. Your own constituent strand-minds are not homogenous *within* themselves any more than all of them, considered as part of your person-mind, are homogenous *among* themselves. And a moment's thought will show you that it must be this way, as anything else would imply an absolute separation.

But—would it? A relative separation I agree, but absolute?

If you think group-mind are most abstract or most developed or most anything, and strand-mind least so, you are setting up a vertical separation. The complication we are introducing here is a complication only because the physical brain *will* persist in analogizing to the 3-D model that it knows, and we must correct for the bias. But the really important theme we have introduced is that choice determines substance. And of that, much more to come.

More on The Porous Nature of Consciousness

Human intelligence is actually the meeting point of many kinds of minds. It is very difficult to say sequentially (that is, in words, which only function one after the other) what is better perceived simultaneously, right-brain fashion. If we could *show* you, you'd see that a whole lot of words are going to be expended to describe something pretty simple. It's the old blind man and elephant thing. In this case the blindness is not because you are in the body but because you cannot intuit what is to be conveyed, but must laboriously construct from what we must equally laboriously describe, feature by feature. This obviously results in redundancy, as we have to go back time and time again to the same things and say, "oh, but now look how this relates to this new thing." A picture in this case would be worth about a hundred thousand words, not just one thousand. But—we hear you say—enough complaining, on with the show.

Only smilingly.

We know. Very well. In all this, we proceed from, and keep returning to, your person-mind, of which you are the ringmaster. We began by pointing out that you incorporate strand-minds, but not every strand-mind is a former person-mind. (Besides, "former" is a time-oriented word that distorts the relationship.) You as ringmaster have to balance and harmonize various strand-mind components as best you can. The degree to which you—to which anyone—is aware of the comprising elements varies, from those who think themselves one unvarying thing, to those who think themselves one thing subject to moods and circumstances, to those who begin to suspect that they are influenced by complexes and compulsions etc. below the level of their awareness, to those who see themselves as blessed or cursed by the presence of other spirit entities, to those whose very sense of identity seems to hang on a thread among competing spirits, or minds, or personalities, however they conceptualize them. (To some they will be past lives, to others, contending spirits, to others personality fragments, depending, as we say, upon what they have been taught implicitly or explicitly, and what is most congenial to their habitual thought patterns.)

But of course this is merely one level of the things affecting your life. All the mechanisms that go into maintaining your body as a machine are another level, and again consciousness of these mechanisms varies widely among different people. Some never given them a thought. They want their body to do something and it does it or can't do it; it gives them health or illness partly depending on whether they follow the rules of good health and partly unpredictably. If something gets out of whack, they try to fix it themselves, or have some health specialist fix it, but in either case they never waver in their assumption that problem and cure are mechanical and nothing more. At the other end of the scale are people who are in continuous communication with their body's intelligences. They balance so readily as to need spend little or no time at it. We will not take the time to fill in the dots; we have sketched it for you years ago in our description of the different levels of control of health that may be obtained by different levels of awareness. But what we did not go into then, and shall here, is what is being communicated with. At the time, we left untouched your assumption that you were communicating with your body's intelligence either as a whole or as special areas, as, a shoulder. There was no reason to get into theory, and good reason to not do so, not wanting to lay out an extensive background. We will not sketch them today. That is the next level of detail down. Today is an overview.

Beyond the conscious strand-lines and the (so far unspecified) minds that maintain the physical organism, other kinds of mind enter in, as well.

I must say, I can't imagine what they could be.

If you could, there wouldn't be much use in your and our going to so much work, would there? We'll say it again: Our work is to relate this to that, when you have been familiar with the this and familiar with the that, but haven't ever thought to relate the two. Either thought or revelation consists in seeing new relationships when previously one saw only separation. Since you can't easily *think* your way to some things, the easy way is to have them *revealed* to you; then it is up to you, to tie the revelation to the rest of your mental world.

That's an interesting thought in itself.

Yes, isn't it? But, to continue. You as human are an intersection of physical and mental and spiritual. Now here is where your readers are going to face amazingly strong resistances, worrying that they are to be led down the garden path, perhaps because of Frank's personal agenda, as you have already seen. But the positive spin on that is, merely, if no resistances, not much new can have been said.

To rephrase: If the material doesn't jolt us out of our accustomed mental habits from time to time, it can't be accomplishing much.

That's what we said. So, the spiritual, and this will complete our overview of the three *kinds* of intelligences that are available to any person-group. (Freudians might consider comparing this to ego, id, and superego, but we warn you that it won't fit at all well.)

Spiritual influences may be looked at as non-physical influences, if you wish, but this is a dumbing-down of understandings that the world's religions have long held and worked out in some detail. If you think angels are fairy-tales but the guys upstairs are sources of valuable information, this doesn't show that you are modern, rational, and clear-sighted. It shows that you are still locked in to a system that sees the world as fundamentally material with perhaps a saving grace of non-material mental presence. If, instead, you think angels are a prettification of demons or nature-spirits or such-like, this is a different problem of assimilation, but probably less of a problem than the previous example. And, lastly, if you think angels are the conventional representation of beings with wings, all sugar-coated and "nice" this is a misunderstanding at the opposite extreme from the first example.

Spiritual forces are *real*, they are *primary*, and they are (therefore) everyday ordinary part of real life.

What we have said will do for a beginning. You have three levels of very different kinds of influence, what may be called human, material, and spiritual, but they may as easily be categorized in entirely different ways. You will notice, Frank, that you earlier confused physical spirits (let's call them) and spiritual spirits, if that isn't too awkward a phrase, thinking they must be the same thing because both non-physical. *[Nature spirits versus TGU, would be a better way to put it.]* But in the first case there really isn't anything you can experience that isn't partly physical in some way. But we have to take that back immediately, for it is true that spiritual influences may be experienced by your minds that are nonphysical (else how are you receiving this, by the way?) but it is a tangled subject, best taken up in its own place, the description in greater depth of spiritual influence.

Now, in this case, someone versed in the lore of nature-spirits would be better able than you to translate what we will say about that level. But such translations will follow from others: We need to give you the outline as best we can, so as to make old things new again.

Continual Internal Interaction

[A friend had given me the complete set of DVD's of the original Star Trek TV series, from the 1960s. I had been connecting with Ernest Hemingway repeatedly and extensively during much of the year 2010, and since he would know what I know, I asked him what he thought of the Star Trek universe. Unexpectedly, I got an insight into our dual perspective on our lives.]

You're coming to them backwards, so I am too. You know the movies, so I know what you know. You never watched the TV show, so it's all seen in retrospect by you, hence by me. (It would be a different experience, my watching it through someone else's mind.) So, like you, I see these young skeletally thin actors through the lens of the older, bulkier actors they would become. So we know something they don't know. We also know of the success after failure of the whole Star Trek concept; we know the interaction and growth of the characters and the increased complexity of the storylines and messages and yet we are seeing them when they didn't know it themselves. *But their non-physical selves did!* You see?

That's how we live our lives.

There's a continual interaction between the physical, living each moment of time, and the non-physical, aware of the overall pattern in ways the individual in the moment can never have the data to share. Yet the non-physical will help the physical to greater awareness if that's part of the pattern. It is in this sense that you can talk about "planning" your lives. Everything people have said about the non-physical patterning of your lives is true from a certain direction—and that direction must come with an awareness of the effects of a different continuing experience of time and the effects of time.

Chapter Four

Living Connected

"[It is no little thing] to achieve anything in any art, to stand alone perhaps for many years, to go a path no other man has gone, to accept one's own thought when the thought of others has the authority of the world behind it,…to give one's life as well as one's words which are so much nearer to one's soul to the criticism of the world."
—W.B. Yeats, *Autobiographies*

One of the toughest roots of all evil is unconsciousness, and I could wish that the saying of Jesus, "Man, if thou knowest what thou doest, thou art blessed, but if thou knowest not, thou art accursed, and a transgressor of the law," were still in the Gospels, even though it has only one authentic source. It might well be the motto for a new morality.
—Quoted in *Jung's Contribution to Our Time*, by Eleanor Bertine, p 57

Communication across the Veil

In any communication process, there is an implicit comparison to radio, or perhaps television. This allows more elaborate and nearly tactile analogies to be used than could have been used before the day of long distance wireless transmission and reception. And, as you know, analogy is the best conveyancer of an abstract idea. (Best, if used as analogy; worst, if used as literal description.) So, let's look at communication in the absence of physical contact.

An *analogy*, remember.

Consider yourselves [to be] receiving sets. You pay attention to the TV—no, let's revert to an earlier day and use the analogy of shortwave radio, to remove the nuance of prepared content. You have a shortwave radio that you could listen to. When you do, you can hear static, and indistinguishable sounds, and garbled fragments, and clear speech, depending. If you don't receive clearly, sometimes it's because your set is faulty, or badly maintained. Sometimes the atmospheric conditions aren't right. Sometimes you can't hear well because you're half asleep, or your head is clogged with the residue of a head cold or sinuses or something. Sometimes the transmitter has his or her own problems, and so even though you are alert and your instrument is tuned and ready and the atmospheric conditions are good, there's nothing coming through. Maybe they're asleep on the other end, for all you know.

Now, when you do receive clearly, what do you receive? Sometimes it is a clearly understandable message from someone you are familiar with—a friend, say, that either you met in the body at some time or perhaps never met except virtually, via the shortwave, but still established diplomatic relations with because of a compatibility. Or perhaps you receive a clear message—that is, the words are clear—that doesn't make a lot of sense to you, and you need to ask for clarification. And sometimes you receive messages, clear or confusing, complete or fragmentary, from unknown sources, and you have to try to deduce the character of the sender by the qualities of the message. (This is what you do every day of your lives, of course. How else do you weigh and measure each other but secondhand?) Sometimes you suspect, or sometimes realize, that you are being misled, deliberately or accidentally. Sometimes you suspect that the person on the other end of the line is crazy, or anyway deluded. And of course if you are communicating with someone whose primary language isn't the same as yours, the possibilities for mis- or non-communication expand significantly, with the additional complication that such misunderstandings may be hidden within seeming clarity. That is, the receiver receives exactly the words the sender sent—but the same word means very different things to each, either because of colloquial differences or misunderstanding on one end or the other of the other's usage. You see.

Beyond these difficulties is the primary obstacle, which doesn't even appear to be there, which is that on either or both ends precision in language may be unknown. The sender sends *more or less* what s/he means, the receiver understands *more or less* what was meant, because the receiver settles for a fast impression rather than really considering the message. Or—on the opposite extreme—the receiver misunderstands because so respectful of the process of transmission that s/he takes literally what is meant as explanatory metaphor, or takes seriously what was meant as a joke, or processes through various distorting filters what is meant as straightforward communication. None of this makes for easy transmission and reception of ideas.

All right. Now, suppose as well as a shortwave radio our person [who is] receiving messages also has a telephone. In the old days before the veil thinned (to mix metaphors), the phone was a land-line, requiring séances or specialized oracles. Today you work with cell phones and anybody can use them anywhere, even while doing three other things. Pursuing this analogy has its interesting aspects. For one, the cell phone appears to be quite different from a shortwave radio, but of course it is actually a form of radio itself, only tied more closely to a physical support network (the cells and towers and their support network of electricity and maintenance). This has its analogy to your communication person-to-person. Each person seems to be accessed directly—through physical means of the senses—and yet each is actually maintained by, and entirely dependent upon, a non-physical infrastructure.

Leaving off that complication for the moment, perhaps it is clear that telephone connections will be clearer than shortwave radio sometimes, under some conditions. Of course if the phone goes out for reasons of interference by any of a thousand physical reasons, shortwave is viable and goes from being a backup to being the primary link. And in any case, shortwave has its own charms and fascinations among hobbyists regardless whether the phone is working. For one thing, it allows communication with those whose phone connection no longer functions.

The story of your time is the gradual extension of such short-wave communication to larger and larger numbers of people, destroying their isolation and leading to an entirely different way of living.

The Conscious and Unconscious Minds

There is a way to avoid spatially-based analogies, though at first it may startle you. Rather than thinking Downstairs/Upstairs or This Side/Other Side, try thinking in terms of Conscious/Unconscious. We—The Guys Upstairs, the inhabitants of The Other Side—are actually a part of you, as you know. But it would be more accurate and would have more explanatory value to begin to think that *you* are part of *us*. Just as the unconscious is vastly larger, wiser, longer-lived and free of space-time limitations, so are we—for the very good reason that what you have been thinking of as the unconscious is in fact the non-physical part of yourselves—including, we remind you, the mind itself.

You are happiest—anyone is—when the friction is least between your conscious life and your unconscious life. It is time for the various analogies about the nature of man to come together when they are describing the same thing, and diverge when they are describing different things. At present they merely blur, or overlap, because it is not realized that they are alternate descriptions. If the nature of mankind in the world is again seen in an integrated manner, through a cultural viewpoint that is broad enough, so many different pieces will fall into place. The anxiety of your times is the unbearable tension of a world that doesn't make sense except in bits. Realizing once more that the physical is an integral part of the non-physical is a huge step toward recovering your balance.

"As above, so below" is the key to many things, and it's why people repeat it even not having the slightest idea why they do, they not knowing what it means. You want to know why "as above, so below"? Because anything else *implies separation.*

Think about that. Anything else implies that on this side of the line, life is one way, but on that side, it is another way. A physical analogy might be—below ground versus above ground, or land versus ocean, or earth-atmosphere versus outer space. Your physical existence is full of boundaries, some realer or more definite than others, but always reinforcing the illusion of separation into units. But the world—that is, reality—is not like that. In reality, not even the barrier between physical and non-physical is what it appears from your end.

Everything, from lowest to highest, is another iteration of the same scheme. Everything is suffused with life because *there is nothing else.* There is no dead-ness to the universe, no "dead matter" into which "life" is inserting itself, contrary to George Bernard Shaw's fable. And there is no level of being that is in pieces that can be (or theoretically could be) detached.

Anything, looked at under the strongest microscope, reveals itself to be not solid but porous. Anything, looked at through the largest telescope, reveals itself not to be chaotic and unrelated to the rest, but patterned and interrelated. The skies—that is, the heavens, the galaxies and universes and nebulae etc.—are as much a solid as the table you write on. The table is as much a wilderness of space connected in regular solid patterns as those same nebulae. And so you in the body as well. "Man is the measure of all things," not only physically but non-physically, because that is the scale of measurement that is most convenient and appropriate *to man.*

We are not confining ourselves to physical appearance or structure—although those analogies *do* apply. For our purposes here, we are pointing out that you extend downward and upward equally; you are part of the microscopic world and the macroscopic world equally. (It ought to go without saying, but doesn't, so we will say it again for completeness, that the entire physical world has its underpinnings in the underlying world, the non-physical world; therefore all manifestation is at the same time an expression of the unmanifest.)

Try to understand, these are not just poetic images, not just philosophic words, but literal if allusive (and elusive) description. If you once receive into yourself the image and feeling of what we are saying here, you will hold it and it will change you. It is in order to do this that we have worked with the concept of the person-group and the social-group, to begin to accustom you to see *how* it can be that you are an expression of continuity with the microscopic and macroscopic worlds, *literally*, both physically and non-physically.

As we "guys upstairs" are part of you but are not confined within any arbitrary grouping, as the molecules of your body at any given time are part of you and then not part of you, seamlessly, as you breathe and cells die and are born and bits of air are breathed in and out, so you, considered as a sort of metaphorical unit, are neither really bounded nor defined. Your constituent organs are actually collections of person-groups at a lower level. You are actually part of person-groups at a higher level. And just as your constituent groups function—*relative to you!*—at a lower, more automatic level, so you function relative to the next higher level—and so correspondingly up and down the scale.

What we have just said is enough. It is the entire key, once understood. Everything we add to it is only because it will not be understood at any given time by any given person according to any predictable schedule.

A Tangled Question

All right friends, I'm ready and willing. Who do I have the honor of speaking to today? Well, "with," not "to." Or, if you have no one special, I'll choose.

You may find it easier to continue your long practice of addressing us as a group unless you wish any one of us, and receiving our communications the same way. We appeared this way for a reason. And perhaps this is as good a time as any to go into it a bit, if only for your book.

The question of guidance from what you call "the other side" is not so much a complicated question as it is a tangled one. But we didn't tangle it from over here! It got tangled because of the various competing or overlapping or antagonistic strands of culture on your end.

In times when a culture is dominant—even if it is challenged from outside, it is still dominant within its own area—in such places—

Well, let's go back a bit.

In the simplest situation, an isolated culture knows of no other ways of perceiving the world *and* has no competing ways within its own area *and* has no discordant tradition cutting against the prevailing ways. In such a society, all is consistency. As all think alike, believe alike, perceive alike—therefore it is not difficult for all to act alike. This is about as different from your time-space as can be.

The next level up in terms of a society is one in which any one of those elements is missing. The next up from that, one with two missing. You see.

No neighbors with other ways.

No conflict between tradition and new ways.

No internal strife between competing elements each with its own traditions.

A society that is uniform within, and not conscious of any discord between its practice and that of its ancestors, may have neighbors with different ways. In such case, the neighbors are regarded either with a blend of indifference and tolerance or with active hostility. Thus, the ancient Romans before they became powerful. Thus, the ancient Greek city-states. Thus, the Hebrew tribes, and Indian tribes, and tribes everywhere. We do not mean to *over*-simplify, because of course these societies had gradations—Greek city-states viewed other Greek states differently than they did non-Greeks; Mohammad distinguished between pagans and People of a Book. But as a simple distinction this will hold.

When such a society conquers or for any reason absorbs another people the conquered must become a part of that society—they must have their own niche into which they can be smoothly fitted—or their very existence would shake that society. So, if the society has a niche for slaves, the newly entered may come in as slaves without disturbing anything—unless they maintain their identity in some way over and above being slaves. We suggest that here you will find the key to the function, plight and effect of the Jews as a people—especially when you compare them to "the Jews of Asia"—the Chinese communities within non-Chinese cultures.

Without meaning to, without wanting to, without any say in the matter whatsoever, by their very presence as an unassimilated body within the simple social order, they are destructive to its simplicity. They *push* that society into a new stage of complexity that it may or may not be able to successfully achieve and maintain.

A society that comes to terms with a minority in its midst is one that has gained an advantage in complexity to set against its disadvantage in loss of homogeneity. How each society deals with that new situation defines differences among them.

One way to deal with it is to find a way to graft that presence onto the prevailing story the society tells itself. Jews in a Christian society are precursors of Christ; in a Muslim society, they are one of three communities descended from Abraham; in a secular society (the west, regardless of nominal allegiances, since the 1800s) a disturbing anomaly interfering with (the myth of) coherent nationhood.

Do you see, now, why so many societies are *insane* when they attempt to deal with minorities? They purge, they discriminated, they murder, they exile—why? For economic reasons? Hardly! For religious reasons? Seemingly so, often, but not really. Well, for ideology's sake? Even less likely.

All this happens because the very presence of the minority stretches the culture, distorts it, makes it uncomfortable—seemingly endangers it. Thus, pogroms. Thus, mass murder.

Now add to the disturbing presence of external foreigners and internal foreigners that presence of a contradiction between present practice and tradition. The result is, for instance, 20th century America. This is far from the only example we might seek! But take it as an example and see if it does not well illustrate our point.

America had foreigners of all kinds *within its fold*, but it incorporated them into its myth be thinking of itself as the melting pot. It had foreigners of all kinds *outside its fold*, but there was no way the foreigners could threaten militarily or economically or culturally. So the first crack in the seamless façade was the culture war between those wanting to change to other values and those seeking to retain current nominal values. *Each side* could claim legitimate descent from the past because of America's *revolutionary tradition*—a sort of historic oxymoron. So neither one could be shrugged off as alien. The result is deadly warfare.

By necessity this outline is too short, and glosses over many a complexity and many a difficulty. None the less, it holds, and offers you the key to your society's problem.

The problem is not the removal of one or the other set of proponents. The problem is not the return to simplicity, for a return never happens.

Here is the problem to be solved: How to move from one layer of simplicity *through* layers of complexity to a *new*, more sophisticated, simplicity. This is the puzzle your society has before it. You may solve it, you may not.

We find it difficult to confine any discussion, as you well know. Every subject links up seamlessly with every other subject—in other words, just as, in a sense, there is only one person, so there is only one thought, only one perception, and that is—*everything! This* is the meaning of the Buddha's admonition that every time you make a distinction you make an error. Not that no distinctions are to be perceived, but that no distinction is or ever could be *absolute*.

So—to move back toward the center of what we want to discuss—people perceive guidance differently because their cultural traditions describe it differently. In a homogenous culture the expectations are homogenous. The more complex and self-contradictory the culture—the more competing threads—the more diversity in understanding; the greater the number of images and concepts, many appearing to be entirely contradictory.

[Interruption]

So, angels. Aliens. Saints. Past lives. Various archetypes. The collective unconscious. Power animals. The ancestors. Earth spirits—we could continue, but the point perhaps is made. We will make it more clearly:

Every society "creates" us in its own image. If it is a fragmented, self-warring society, then the gods are at war. If a powerful homogenous society concerned at most with the transgressions of individuals, this is what it will see on the other side. It isn't a chaos over "here"—except in that it is chaos over "there."

You are fighting over competing visions of what you call the afterlife, or the spiritual reality, or the other side, or heaven and hell, or nirvana, or even the energy of the great mindless machine—and you don't see that you are grappling with your own contradictions in the only way you know—by projecting them onto us. Projecting in two senses of the term: projecting, as in "seeing them in others rather than oneself" and as in

Sorry, lost the thread.

Two forms of projection—one, projecting one's inner stuff, two, creating, of that projected material, shapes and beings.

So, if you project warring forces (and no reason you shouldn't; anything that exists, exists on both sides of the veil, being different as we have said mainly according to the laws of the turf involved) those warring forces will be seen as warring *individuals*, or *groups*, because it is too difficult psychologically for you to hold the view of abstracts. Thus the warfare of the good and bad angels. *It is all projection: That does not mean it does not exist.* It means, merely, you cannot see ultimates.

So—here is the point we wish to make at this time. Your quest to understand (and by "you" we mean, at this time, all who read this, sharing the quest) is part of society's work. You are doing invisible mental work that though invisible is not unreal or not important. *It is real work* and there are few enough to do it. Consider the work, if you will, to be that of creating and infusing with energy a visualization, a new archetype, a *container*. Your society is tearing itself apart because you are in the time of new birth. *Aid that birth!*

For clarity—"your society" may now be considered (for the first time in *recorded* history) all the sub-societies of the planet. You are in a global civilization. Is it a surprise that previous containers are not adequate?

Those who cannot create rely upon those who can. It requires much less to adhere to a new vision than to obtain and co-shape it. Your work is to help to shape the vision so that your fellows—many of whom will hate you for the work!—may benefit.

It is a great and rare privilege to participate in the coalescing of a new civilization; rarer to participate in a new *form of* civilization; rarest of all—your fate—to also participate in the coming to consciousness of a new way of being human.

So. This is a coherent place to pause. Type this and send it off to the winds as before. And as always you have our thanks for participating in the work.

And you know you have mine; this greatly enriches my life.

Using Guidance

My friends, what have you to say about my blog, or self development by choice, or past lives, or your ongoing project working through me, or the price of eggs?

The more pointed the question, remember, the more pointed the answer. However, we take your question to be in effect "what is the thing you would most like me to know and perhaps to communicate today?"

Close enough. And the answer is?

We realize that it seems irresponsible even to you for you to be blogging without consideration of how that is to translate into income for you. But the operative word, as you like to say, is "seems." What is practical and what is not depends upon many factors, most of them hidden from you most of the time. That is why it is practical to rely upon the guidance, once you have sorted out your issues around "is it me downstairs or is this guidance?"

You are separated by *time* and by *space* and by the shell (call it) between yourself and any other. All of those things make it harder for you to calculate. How do you factor into your calculations things that are going to happen to you in the future—next month, say—that have cast no shadow before them? How can you take into account things happening across the world from you—or across the street!—that you don't know about? How can you predict what others are doing, thinking, feeling that may lead them to affect your life?

The short answer is, you *can't*.

The somewhat longer answer is, you *can* to some degree, by tuning your awareness—by "remote viewing" your life, so to speak. But you've seen how fragmentary a process that is. Why not do it the easy way and rely on the part of you that isn't confined in one bit of time and space? And that is what guidance is—the course-corrections that are offered you from a perspective that takes into account the things that you can't see or sense.

Why would you need guidance to help you count your spoons? You wouldn't. The data is at your fingertips. But guidance is awfully handy when you need to get a hint as to which way to turn—which thread to follow—when the answer can't be calculated by rational means.

And after all, what are hunches but spurts of accepted guidance? What is luck, but unconscious living in accordance with guidance?

A very persuasive case, if I needed persuading. I will pass it on, of course.

You have come to a new way of being that is firmly rooted in the old. That is the only way that grafting works. Without firmly rooted stock, there is no base for the new to get its grip on life. That is the difference between your specific task and the task of others—psychics for instance. They can do it but they can't *not* do it, they can't *remember* not doing it, they can't be frustrated by being unable to do it—and so they can't be the bridge. You—among many others—can.

Yes that is what I am consciously attempting to do on my blog.

Of course. You of your own knowledge—which means to your reader "maybe *I* can get my *own* knowledge and judge whether he is right or wrong." And when they get good at it they'll realize that it is "when he is right and when he is wrong" (that is, that no one is infallible) and they'll maybe escape Psychics Disease.

You gentlemen have any more to say about things?

It's up to you, really. We are always available, and we tend to lend you a sense of urgency when we need you to do something timely.

Yes, I have figured that out, finally. Of course, under the circumstances I get suspicious of impulses. Yet as I have no objection to doing your bidding, I act even when suspicious of whose idea it is. I expect due credit at least for being willing to be a dupe if need be.

Cat's-paw.

Whatever. In my case, preparing so many past sessions to be postings has revived my interest in doing morning sessions, as I did in 2005-06 [when I enjoyed five months of conversations with Joseph Smallwood]. But I think that rather than resume with Joseph I will take advantage of my increased access—and I see now why you prompted me with that bright idea—to talk to others at the same depth if possible. If anything it should be easier so long as we stay away from factual matters that may be checked.
But—whom? Joseph the Egyptian comes first to mind, but then I think of Bertram, and John. Do any of you or all of you have a

preference? What am I saying, of course you have a preference, and you are leading me like a tethered donkey. But that's fine, let's go. Proceed, friends.

We do approve your attitude—including your levity. An attitude of skepticism, or of true-believer-ism, or of excessive reverence, or of insistence that certain fences must be absolutes and remain absolutes, would make all this far harder for you. Such attitudes have their advantages, and are worked out in other personalities, but you have found a style that works well for you.

So who is up?

[Joseph, the Egyptian from long ago] Your mind and mine run more closely together than you might expect if you considered only the great difference in our backgrounds. "Separated" as we are by gulfs of time and space, in cultures that make our very way of experiencing the world nearly incommunicable one to the other, if it were not for the threads we share we could speak only through chains of intermediaries, each of which would necessarily (by his very function) increase miscommunication. I am the source of much of what in you is so strange to your companions. My way in the world is to a great extent your way, and it is very far removed from what has been common in your world.

I lived in a high point in the culture that lived in the Two Kingdoms. You live in what seems to be a high point in your civilization. Yet how different your circumstances from mine! I was a part of the civilization; you are a dissenting seed.

That is badly said. Let me set the idea more firmly in your mind, and you will be able to better translate it. [Pause] You see? *I* was *maintaining. You,* in representing and fostering the same value as an orientation, are *revolutionizing.* My times supported what I am. You came into being (with so many others) to turn your society to something that will support what you are. The working out of this requires that you—and so many others—in effect be born into exile. When you came of age (at about seven; that is, when you had formed a soul and were ready for an injection of spirit that would orient you to your life's task) you realized unconsciously that you were not in congenial surroundings. We are not criticizing your parents or family or immediate circumstances, we mean that you were formed to fit into a society that did not exist, and you felt the divergence by your own inability to fit in to what existed. This does not refer to transient difficulties but to your fundamental orientation in the world.

This is an unavoidable if painful accompaniment to a life that is intended to break new ground. You could fit in or you could not. If you fit, then every movement toward what would come into being would be a painful stretch. If you did not fit, then every movement in the right direction would reduce the stretch, would be a clear indicator that it *was* the right direction.

This is said to you and for you, but also to and for so many others who have lived their lives in painful exile. It wasn't accidental, it wasn't unnecessary, and it wasn't fruitless. But the working out of it is *now!* It is what you are moving *toward*. It is not a resting place but a vector. And I smile as I know that you don't *quite* know what a vector is, but I use it through you because at some level you do know it—think of it as motion or inertia in one given direction. Your technical friends will cringe but that is close enough for our purposes. You are not going to be as comfortable standing still as you will be moving in the one indicated direction. And what direction is that? The one you are inclined to move in! That is what guidance is, you know, a pointer toward the right direction for you.

Hmm. I'm pretty tired already and it isn't 10 a.m.

No need to wear yourself out—great need to not wear yourself out, in fact. Steadfastness, not spurts and inconstancy. But steadfast does not mean unceasing, only unchanging in intent.

Thank you, Joseph. My correspondent says Joseph means "God's servant" which I like very much.

We can all be Joseph. It is our choice.

Deepening Access

Guidance shapes your lives, necessarily and for no one's benefit more than your own! So the trick is *not* to develop new access. It is *not* to come into contact with forces or beings who may be requested to aid you. It is simply to do more consciously what you cannot help doing in many ways, in many times, unconsciously.

You breathe. If you did not breathe, you could not live. Yet you may go to a self-development class, or a meditation class, and find that the first step is to learn how to breathe properly. That is—how to breathe *consciously*. The process, the necessity, the reward, is similar here. You live in guidance. Now, learn to do it consciously.

Now, when your teacher taught you how to breathe consciously, did s/he have to move your muscles for you? Was it necessary to give each person individual, highly detailed, instruction? Was it necessary to *study* the subject? *Wasn't most of the instruction accomplished when the teacher pointed out to you that you could and should breathe consciously?*

Techniques can be important, but we say this flatly: *Technique is detail.*

No one ever became a great artist or a great saint or a great intellectual or a great *anything* by mastering technique. Greatness does not inhere in technique but in inspiration. Craft, skill, proficiency, relate to technique, and the truly great were not deficient in technique, but no one has ever done or ever will do anything great and lasting and important and soul-lifting on technique alone.

This is where religions may go wrong. Their hearts may be in the right place but their confidence may be misplaced, thinking that technique—rules—the following of rules, the doing a certain thing in a certain manner—is the way. It is not. It may be the method to be followed along the way, but it is not the way.

This is where art goes wrong. One proficient in technique and not in touch with guidance produces soul-less (literally!) trash. One who is connected may produce soaring art even with defective technique—in fact he will create his own technique as a by-product of expressing that inspiration.

Similarly, your readers. It does not matter how guidance is made conscious, provided that the heart is pure; that is, that the intent is pure.

But having said that, we need to take back a bit of it—even though what we just said is true. And the reason to modify the statement is the existence of fear. Fear is the great distorter.

All we have to offer was offered by Jesus and could be restated in those words. It is a matter of interpreting into modern language. And the reason it needs doing is the *fear* that people have—the fear of making a mistake that will damn them, not a negligible fear, as you know first-hand from your Catholic boyhood—that may lead them to lash out against what would be a message of hope and promise. That fear needs to be recognized and honored; their own internal guidance will do its part.

We are *not* saying—do not mis-hear us, friends—we do *not* say that opposition stemming from fear may always be overcome; neither do we suggest that guidance will always lead people along similar paths. As odd as it may seem to you, other paths that may seem utterly inconsistent with following guidance have their place too. God is not necessarily agreeing with you and disagreeing with them! Each person's path has been chosen—is *being* chosen—and for you to convert them is the same process as them converting you: good intention but perhaps an invasion. God is at Gateway courses *[at The Monroe Institute]*—but he is equally at Baptist church services, and Muslim mosques and—though you may hate to think it—Pat Robertson's television broadcasts.

We are straying from our point which is that all have access to guidance but that fear may prevent some of you from making that access more conscious.

Treat that fear as you would treat any obstruction in the flow of energy: Make it conscious (that is, bring it into aware-ness), dwell in it (that is, absorb the character of it; *feel* it and feel its nature) and reason with it (ask how it is serving you, *listen* to the response, and either tell it that you don't need that protec-tion or, if appropriate, suggest another way that the same kind of protection may be provided without interfering with your development of greater access to conscious guidance).

Make it conscious.

Dwell in it.

Reason with it.

That is the way to deal with all obstructions, be they physi-cal, mental, emotional or energetic. Enough for now.

Consciousness as Movement

You taught yourself how to deal with the physical and emo-tional problems of others by envisioning the forces in play as doing what they thought was right for the individual, but doing it mindlessly, repetitively, and so at last inappropriately. You learned how to reprogram those robots, and learned, through the experience of your friends as you worked with them, that not only could reprogramming stop negative behavior, it could be redirected to positive channels. Our point here is to redefine your robot analogy in light of fluctuating and porous conscious-ness. You must for the moment regard your consciousness as not a *thing*, not solid in any way, not permanent. Your *consciousness* is not the same thing as *you*, any more than the volatile and temporary contents of a computer's RAM are the same thing as the computer, or as the computer's software.

There is nothing permanent about a state of consciousness, because it is not designed to be permanent, and could not do what it does if it were permanent. One permanent state of consciousness would be the equivalent of a computer locking up. Consciousness *fluctuates*. It is *supposed* to. It was *designed* to. It is in those fluctuations that it expresses the fluctuation of the forces exerted upon it from various and changing agents including external circumstances, the nature of the given moment, the effective pressure of other consciousnesses, and the effective participation of its strands and group-mind, moment to moment. If we weren't pressed for time, we would repeat this, because it is important. Indeed, in stating it here, now, we *do* repeat, for we have said it before.

If, instead of identifying with your momentary state of consciousness, you realize that it is an interim summing-up of your life at that moment (for so it may be seen) or as the result of your past choices (for it may be seen that way, too) or as the interplay of your known and unknown inner and outer components (a third way it may be seen), you will see both how at the mercy of other forces your daily life is and how vast an array of abilities you may command merely by realizing the fact.

There is a lot packed into that paragraph, and we advise that you re-read it more than once, and wrestle with it until (in connection with your ever-helpful guys upstairs, of course) you have anchored it to your practical everyday life. Ultimately it will ground and anchor many a free-floating concept, rendering the whole more coherent and usable.

As to porousness. Again, you must let go of the idea that *you* are the unit you think yourself, any more than that your emotional makeup is the same at age 8 and 15 and 28 and 60. It just isn't so, and the attempt to see as consistent and unitary what is neither can only be made by slurring over all the detail and by resolutely forgetting vastly more than you remember. And this is what is customarily done, of course, but it does not serve you.

Remember that your consciousness at any given moment is the person-mind comprising many strand-minds and participating in a group-mind. This, remember, is over-simplification, but it is complicated enough until you have anchored the concept among your other mental orienting concepts; perhaps later we can then add nuance and exception and complication.

But what is true for your person-mind is also true for the group-mind of which you are a strand-mind, and equally true for the strand-minds that make up your person-mind. Again—always—as above, so below.

Therefore all is movement, and change, and interaction—and is this not your experience of life? This porousness is why and how you do not stagnate. At one and the same time, life is freedom and fate, and it does not depend upon viewpoint in this case. That is, we are not saying that life may be viewed as freedom *or* fate, depending upon the point of view. We are saying, instead, it is both, always, in the same way that there cannot be an up and no down, or an inner and no outer. The two—freedom to create; being created with—are inextricably linked because *the same*. If you pull on a string, the string also pulls you.

Yes, we can quit again for the moment. Although this morning session is shorter than usual, when added to the middle-of-the-night session it will give quite enough for your friends to chew on as they begin their day, or whenever they come to it.

Our Work

We are more or less at the point where you need to do the work of summarizing the past few sessions so as to hold it more in your mind. This sharpens *your* focus which makes it easier to sharpen our focus.

Care to expand upon that?

You might look out at this way. We have said, your limited RAM forces you to try to make efficient use of symbols if you are to be able to hold complex associations in mind long enough—simultaneously enough—for you to process them. Writing does that by substituting permanence—or, we should say, persistence—for momentary awareness. But as you *absorb* information, as you *process* it and make what was new into an accustomed part of your mental library, you—in effect—cease to need RAM to process that particular information, and can therefore associate it with new information. You understand?

You only absorb new material, beyond a certain point, by having previously absorbed and assimilated the material received previously.

That's right. And material received in right-brain fashion particularly requires left-brain processing, for it will not have received it in the way information received in other ways would have been received. You know from your experience that information given out in this way does not go into short-term memory unless recalled via conversation or via re-hearing from a recorder or re-hearing from a written record. But—more than that—neither you nor anyone reading this will be able to absorb this material by reading it and then going on to other things. *It is to be thought about*—not remembered, certainly not memorized, but thought about—so as to incorporate it. We'll say a couple of words about that.

Your mind, we have said, is in the non-physical, and your brain in the physical. While you are functioning in the body your access to information must be filtered to you in one of two ways (usually, in both, actually, but that would not assist the analysis, so we will proceed for the moment as if only one or the other). You may receive *intuitively*—that is, directly, without the interference or intermediation of thought processes—or you may receive *sensorially*, which for our purposes at the moment (not forever) we are going to define as employing the habits of cognition.

You mean, I take it, by association or deduction or induction. But why call that sensorially? I recognize, you want an opposite to intuitive, but is that the proper opposite term in this case?

We are open to suggestion, as you say.

Well why not simply oppose intuition to thought? "Thought" could include induction, deduction and association, surely.

We'll accept that scheme, subject to later correction if necessary. It overlooks for the moment the part that your sensory apparatus plays in what seems to you a process of thought unconnected to the senses, but we can always discuss that at another time. Make a note.

So, then, intuitive and thought-filtered reception. If you come to a new place via thought processes, the procedure itself will assure that the new material associates with the old, at least in the context in which it occurred to you. You study a subject, you learn it by systematizing your knowledge in one way or another. If, though, instead of studying systematically, you receive a thought (for that is how it seems to us, reception rather than production, for you should not take the credit for that which you did not deliberately produce) that does not have any context but the one that produced it—if it is what you call a "stray thought"—you will probably lose it, perhaps forever, if you do not in some way associate it with other thoughts beyond the momentary context. This, after all, is a main function of a journal, to store such thoughts against a later time in which they will find another more permanent or more significant context.

Such stray thoughts are not what we mean by intuitive reception, however similar to it they may be. They share the quality of evanescence, but they are received via a quite different process. In fact, that word "process" well describes the difference.

You are, in your left-brains, word *processors*. You process sequentially, first this, then this, then this. It is the nature of the left-brain.

In your right-brain (typically; not of course universally or even strictly speaking, but as a useful generalization) you process non-verbal gestalts; entire irreducible relationships; things that can only be grasped whole if they are to be grasped at all. Landscapes, photographs, road maps (disregarding the processing that must follow the initial reception of the spatial relationships).

For the purposes of illustration, the right-brain material may be looked at as that which is more easily grasped than expressed, and, for that matter, more easily felt than grasped. There is nothing more fleeting than an unexpressed, on absorbed, feeling. Nothing but direct intuition.

The work you are doing in studying material that has been received intuitively is the associating of its component ideas into a coherent system for yourselves, so that it may be fitted into the rest of your lives. Else, what good to you could it be? It might serve as encouragement, true, but it could not do much beyond that. If it is to transform your life, it will do so by transforming your *mental* life. And this it can do only if you do the work of absorbing it and its implications.

What we are saying here is only common sense and common experience. You never own anything until it has become a part of you, and this never happens until you take it into yourself. Doing the work of sitting with new material, absorbing the "feel" of it, and thinking about it, and applying it, is the price you must pay if it is to be yours.

I heard, more or less between the lines, that everybody is going to hear something different in this material, that no two people are going to construct the same mental model.

No, and how could they? It is in the association with the rest of your life that this material is made yours. Given that by design everyone's life is very different, how could or should the end-result be the same in any two instances? But—that is not a weakness but a strength. Just as variety in plants is safer than genetic monotony, so variety in the application of insights is more reliable, more versatile, more enduring, then any lockstep memorized catechism could be. It is in the unvarying adoption of uniform expression of thought, that thought dies. What is as dead and deadening as petrified thought? Be, instead, *living* wood, growing, assimilating, connecting sky and earth and the deep underground.

Nice image.

We've done this before.

Complementary Advantages

It is in 3D Theater that you have your best chance to shape yourselves, mold yourselves—not surprisingly, as *that is what it is for!* Association with unlike others, and delayed consequences (or what might be called persistence of form) allow and encourage and almost but not quite require that you spend your lives choosing (if only be default) what you will be. What you *begin from* is not under your 3D control, but all else *is*. Laugh at anyone who denies free will—s/he is using free will in choosing to be persuaded by whatever factors convince him or her that free will does not exist.

On this side, though, we have neither constraints of one-time-one-place in the same way you do (ours exists in a different way) or delayed consequences (again, we experience it, but radically differently, as we have explained other-when).

Because the field upon which we live is so different from yours, you and we offer each other complementary advantages.

We can give you broader perspectives, and can facilitate communication regardless of space and time. *You* can put us into spaces we cannot go ourselves, or can go only very laboriously and indirectly, and then not often or long.

As always it takes us many words to say the simplest things not because we are not pointed consciousness but because we cannot see how to make a true or helpful statement without at least sketching in some minimal context.

Here goes.

If you, in a body, interact with someone no longer in a body—as you easily can by the thoughts and emotions you feel for them, about them—and the prayers or curses you will to send them—*you can affect who they are*; which affects what kinds of others they now gravitate toward, or feel comfortable with. The language dictates concepts like "change" and "movement" and we don't have time—you don't have time, this Monday morning—to correct the mistaken nuance. Just remember that nearly everything that can be said is analogy.

If you forgive someone, or if you so act as to elicit forgiveness from someone, the connections between the sides are to that extent altered. If there has been a chain of hatred, say, you on your side feel it as thought it were "merely" psychological. We on our side experience it as an external constraint. That's perhaps the best way to put it. By altering those bonds you *move* us—you allow us to move—in a much more real and nearly tangible way than you commonly suspect.

What are prayers for the dead, but the offering of energy to them that will allow them to "move" higher—*they themselves being relatively helpless to change what they are*, once they leave a body.

Our Lives As Ringmasters

It's well and good to say that the individual is a convenient fiction—in order to erode false absolutes in your thinking—but still you live, and you know yourselves as more than flow, more individual than identical molecules in an ocean.

Time for a corrective, then.

Yes, but remember that when we change viewpoints it is to illuminate another side of the subject; it is not to un-say what we said before that may be contradicted by a new viewpoint.

So, until now we have been concentrating on the threads rather than the containers. Don't now throw all that overboard when we begin to look at the rings instead of the strings.

You come into life to be the ring-master of many elements, each of which is itself in the process of continuous flux in the same way and for the same reason. Does this not shed light on why life is so complex and continuously changing? It isn't just a matter of astrology, of different celestial influences on an otherwise unchanging individual. It isn't just sociology, at the other end, a matter of the patterns set up around you by your environment. And it isn't just psychology, between the two, a matter of mind in an environment, although this is closest.

It is as common sense would suppose, only the unit is vastly more porous than is commonly supposed.

Remember always—perhaps we don't stress this strongly enough or often enough—it isn't that we are providing you with new material as much as a new way of putting together the pieces. So you will find bits in Seth or in Gurdjieff or anywhere and suddenly the connection will snap into place and you will see what was being said that you couldn't, previously, ground in your life. And of course it will work the other way, as well. Something another body of information offers will explain what we provide here.

Now, you are in a body as ring-master of all these elements, aware of them to greater or lesser extent. At one level of consciousness all things seem part of you and you of them, and no meaningful separation presents itself. This is the infant before it forms an "I" relative to the rest of the world—and it is the individual awareness *after* it has gone through the perception of separation between the I and the other—more or less what you're getting to now, conceptually. In the long meantime, your relationship with all those elements varies all over the place. Sometimes you are not very aware of forces beyond your definition of your consciousness and other times you are more so. (Besides fluctuations within any one person, there are wide variations between individuals, as should be obvious. Some at their most sensitive to other influences are not nearly as sensitive as others at their least sensitive. Each person-group differs from others in this, as in other things.)

Two Ways of Connecting

You can observe that I have been drawn to the idea of traveling to Egypt, particularly these past few weeks, drawn because the attraction came from out of left field, but one thing has flowed smoothly into another. I need to decide soon if this is something I should do. Any thoughts on the advantages of visiting sacred sites?

You should realize that connecting may be done non-physically, not only physically. Physical visitations are potent awakeners. But if you are ready for awakening, you can visit without carrying your body, and the results *in terms of connecting* will be the same.

I think you are making distinctions I don't quite get.

To go to a sacred site to which you have a known or suspected connection is to leave yourself open to sudden recognitions, as when you visited Salisbury and were in awe of the church tower and recognized that awe as not really "yours," or when you visited the *[London]* embankment and saw the monument marked July

1, 1916 and were flooded with grief that, again, was not quite "yours." This may be said to be the use of physical cues to focus your attention on something that will both release a recognition and allow for the recognition of the recognition. Similarly, to go to a site to which you have no known connection may provide a huge jolt of sudden recognition. Both kinds of experiences are designed to provide new input into your conscious mental processing. But why not do for sacred sites what you do when hunting for someone "over here" to chat with? Why should it be any different? You are using nonphysical means to explore nonphysical connections. To put it bluntly, go or don't go. You will get one thing by going, another thing by not going—if you get anything at all.

This doesn't feel like Joseph.

Good listening. There was a hand-off; it's easier for me to get across the idea; you and I are in closer resonance when it comes to ideas.

All right, David, go ahead.

Thoreau knew how to travel by staying at home and reading, and by seeing what was in front of him and *extrapolating*. "What I got by going to Montréal was a cold," remember.

Not an exact quotation, but I remember.

Well, let's put it in terms of opportunity costs.

I always am glad for that economics course I took.

It's a reason for education in the liberal arts, for certain: you acquire a library of reference points that you may use later if you choose to. All right, using the concept of opportunity costs—that anything you do prevents you from doing something different at the same time—look at traveling. A chart perhaps, either/or:

> Physical movement *or* remaining home
> New sensations *or* no new distractions
> Out of any rut *or* surface life

You will remember, you *needed* to read during your trip. You always have needed to. And you had to flog yourself into moving along and doing things: It isn't your accustomed way.

I remember vividly.

"I have traveled extensively in Concord." Surely you don't think he meant, only, "I know the woods hereabouts thoroughly."

I don't know that I've ever much thought about it.

Well, think about it. He was digging himself in, deeper and deeper, seeing the same things more intensely, deepening his roots in time *and* eternity as best he could. Unlike you he wasn't torn between ambition and inertia nearly as much, and he had more opportunity, sooner, to satisfy (and this means, to sate) what ambition he did have. And so, he knew more what he was about, because he didn't have so many crosscurrents distracting him.

No Internet, too; no telephones or other electronic diversions.

He'd have used them if he'd had them, and would have done so as he did the daily newspapers—as grist for his mill. The important thing is that the mill grind to a purpose.

So I may get something equivalent whether I do or don't go to Egypt, provided I am of the mind to do so.

"Travel is broadening," you know.

I can see that I am a very different person from what I would have been had I not done so much traveling physically and non-physically.

You are very different, too, from what you would have been had you traveled *only* physically or non-physically. But you have done so.

I can see I am not going to feel my way into a yes or no, here, and I don't know that I want to. But it's an interesting exploration into the variables. Thanks.

Perception and Morality

You have begun to see how the abstract concepts you learned in your remote viewing attempt can be applied to larger areas of life. This is very valuable as a corrective against Psychics Disease, against becoming and snarled in conspiracy theories— and against being prone to accept the party line and the official version of things! But it extends beyond that. Some of this will appear obvious, but not everything that is obvious to one will be obvious to another.

Consider. Your scientific outlook, your religious outlook, your anti-scientific or anti-religious outlook, whatever, can *only* be provisional. No matter what you think you know, it can never be absolutely true, and what is true in one context may be untrue in another. Not "seen as" or "seem to be" but actually. It is a matter of precision.

You read a book "long ago" about fractals, remember, and one point made by way of illustration was that no one knows *or can know* the length of the British coastline. The reason, quite simply, is that at each smaller scale of measurement, new discontinuities arise. What is a straight line at a larger scale of measurement is seen to be indented, complicated, at a smaller scale. At a scale still smaller, it gets longer because more irregularities—previously inconsequential and perhaps not even discernible at a larger scale—must be taken into account.

This serves as a good useful example. If no one knows or can know something so simple as the length of a coastline, what can be fixed and absolute?

The same thing goes for values and for moral codes, and for the same reason. Thou shalt not kill may be an absolute for some. For most it is a fixed value but not absolute. Given a condition in which one must kill in order to protect others, the value conflicts with others, and the person caught in the conflict must decide among them. *There is nothing wrong with this* because it cannot be otherwise. Life holds no absolutes. Would you not lie sometimes to protect others even if you would not do so to protect yourself? Would you not steal to feed your starving family?

Do not misunderstand us to be saying that morality is illusory, or that a moral code, a code of ethics, is illusory or futile. Exactly the contrary is our point. *Because* there can be no absolute, *because* all values exist along with others that may at some time conflict with them, *therefore* people need to make their own code (or follow another's) so that they will have a guide when dilemmas arise.

Every society, religion, social group, family, and individual creates a code and lives up to it well or badly. Because any individual comes under many codes, some of them conflicting, each person chooses how to behave, what to value above what in what conditions. An easy example (though not necessarily easy in practice) is family versus the state: where is your first loyalty if it is one against the other? Another is family versus social group, or church versus state. The permutations are endless, as life itself.

You are always responsible for the code you choose to live by. It can be no other way. You may change the code, frequently or rarely or not at all, but you will necessarily have one, and much of it is likely to be beneath your level of consciousness. (Gang members and politicians have codes relating primarily to their peers and colleagues, and any other allegiances will be weighed against these.)

The point, again, is that nothing exists in isolation. Therefore, everything is relative. "Moral relativism" is entirely unavoidable, or are you willing to live and be judged by the moral codes of various classes in Elizabethan England, or Stalinist Russia, or third century Rome, or Aztec Mexico? You could not live by the codes even of a hundred years ago, even if you knew what they were. So—no more thinking that any moral code is or can be "right" and unchangeable. Right and wrong always get mixed together beyond separation, as any policeman or judge can tell you from first-hand experience. As to unchangeable—think of the variances just in what is considered acceptable sexual conduct over the course of 50 years. If that subject is too charged, how about the perceived morality of the business place or stock market or government?

Note well, here we are not discussing how well or badly these codes are followed, but how the code itself adjusts to changing times not because people become more immoral but because their perceptions change as to the morality or otherwise of a given act.

So, you say, "perception versus story"? You think we are far off track. But we would say if you will title this "perception and morality" the connection will appear soon enough. Write this up and think about it, and if you wish more, you know where to find us.

You Shall Be Your Own Interpreters

So we're a long way before daylight, and the fruit stand is open early. Who and why?[Pause] Nothing. All right, let's talk, Papa

[Hemingway]. What is the rule, here? Sometimes I can scarcely get a word in and somebody's off and running. Other times, as now, there's a blankness, a waiting for me to decide what to broach.

Your question contains your answer. That *is* what's going on, a gradual transfer of the initiative. And that's worth a few words.

Suppose we on this side want to get a message across. We have to have willing hands, and we have to have hands that are aware, not merely willing. And it's better yet if the person is knowledgeable—they make a better implement for us to use.

Three levels of qualification, you see: willingness, awareness, prepared ground. Given willingness, we can proceed however strong the difficulties. Given willingness and awareness—that is, given that the willing soul is actually aware that we're trying to come through—we can do far more, far more easily. And given a willing person whose awareness has grown to the extent that they're conscious of our presence, and our intent maybe, we can do even more if that person's background knowledge has some special mass of material that we can use for our purposes, if only to furnish us with material for analogy.

Now, given all that, the material we attempt to bring across is somewhat shaped, somewhat limited, you can see, by the person we are working with. For one person we can come through only as through a blank screen—Edgar Cayce and Jane Roberts went into trance to allow us to dictate chapter and verse. For others, we provide the material in a more or less ordered sequence and the willing scribe records—and wrestles with, and sometimes resists—the material. Neale Donald Walsch, for instance. For still others, we suggest connections and the artist on the other end shapes them into music or paintings or whatever form, and although the material does not have intellectual content, necessarily, it does have the ability to move people in certain ways, neither the artist nor the audience knowing the source or intent of the inspiring force. Jackson Pollock is an example of that, by the way, or Gustav Mahler: thousands more, known or unknown. For still others, Carl Jung for example, a lifetime's intellectual work may be so shaped by intuitive direction as to be said to be continuously inspired, but not particularly consciously *in terms of concept*. That is, the concept may be that he is thinking and digesting experience, while the underlying reality of continuous inspiration may go unnoticed and even (depending on the individual's conscious beliefs) unsuspected. You understand, we intend for all who read these words to apply them to their own lives. The text for the sermon is, "you shall be your own interpreters, and rely upon authority no more." And this has interesting ramifications.

For one, if everybody lives listening to this still small voice, no one's outside authority can be accepted until verified by an inner knowing. Isn't that what we have been saying? Don't accept it unless it resonates within you? For another, if everybody else is listening, your own knowings are to be given in a spirit of humility, no matter how sure you are of your message, for you are one among equals, not one exalted. For yet another, if your source of information is thus as high as you can reach, you have a responsibility to *live* the truth you have been entrusted with. You may or may not be called upon to share it in words, but you will certainly be called upon to live it in deeds. "Knowledge not lived is sin," Cayce said, and we can only agree, sin meaning "missing the mark." And for another, you must listen carefully and with discernment, for greater abilities imply greater responsibility. Adopting any stray thought as if it were the gospel may prove more dangerous and self-defeating than remaining deaf to inspiration. Beware Psychic's Disease.

And the greatest, or should we say the most widespread, difficulty is to not fall into excessive humility and passivity on one hand, or psychic inflation and arrogance on the other. In every way, you should be able to remain balanced. In this as in so many things, Jesus' words may guide you: As he said, you can know the inner nature of a thing by the fruit it bears. If it comes labeled Messages From Heaven and bears fruit like pride, deceit, hardness of heart, isolation from your fellows—that tells you all you need to know. Conversely if it comes wrapped in labels that say Danger! Extreme Weirdness but yields the seven virtues *lived out*, again, that tells you what you need to know.

Now in this we are ignoring the necessity for discerning true messages in eccentric packages, or rather we are blinking the occasional difficulty of taking the true kernel and leaving the eccentric husk without inadvertently distorting or mutilating or truncating the essence—for sometimes what appears foolishness is an integral part of the wisdom, as for instance the psychological wisdom Carl Jung rediscovered came wrapped in Alchemy.

That's all very clear. I think you begin by saying that you're undertaking a gradual transfer of the initiative.

Yes. Once a certain amount of intellectual groundwork has been laid down, a certain type of person is able to move forward in ways he or she couldn't in the absence of a clarifying concept. It is for them that you are writing, of course. Other types are addressed by other willing servants, in other forms of message.

TGU as Expression of Forces

Dr. Jung, reading your ideas about the repressed unconscious breaking out and causing chaos—can we relate that to my guys upstairs?

Any system will have its application to any other system until the limits of analogy causes it to break down. How could two systems dealing with the same aspects of reality not relate to each other? It would indicate that at least one was seriously in error.

The guys upstairs—we guys upstairs, I suppose I must say—are forces, or conduits of forces, as much as they are localized consciousnesses. Over and above whatever one is or does as an individual is what one is or does as a representative of his ancestors—spiritual and physical both. If one is a conduit for vast forces, and those forces cannot <u>flow</u> because there is a dam constructed somewhere on the physical side—well, at some point there is likely to be a collapse and then a flood!

Suppose that you are living your life in a merely conscious, routinized way. You do not get into touch with your "unconscious" aspects, your guys upstairs as they manifest in your life. You seek to conform to a code that may be well-meaning but does not fit your psychology. Your life externally is more or less a rejection, a repudiation, of the internal life that more truly represents you.

Yes, it is true that you can choose, and it is your choice. But it is also true that too long a time spent making bad choices *will* lead to results. For an individual considered as an individual, the stakes may not be too high. What is a frustrated life worth, one may ask. But—pile enough of these dead leaves, and you have the making of a tremendous bonfire. You need, in life, to come to terms with evil, chiefly by seeing that antithetical values nevertheless have their rights. They must be honored, as the sexual forces must be honored or suffered to run disruptively riot. If forces have become embodied, it is *[in order]* that they may be expressed. If too much unbalanced non-expression takes place—too much repression in a certain direction—then to that degree the will of the other side, as mobilized, is being frustrated.

Guidance, Suffering, and the Virtues

Now, to stay with our earlier point, you, Frank, were not so aware of the reactions or motivations or independent life of others because you were blinded by the sun of your own solar system, so to speak. Your contemporaries were more rumor to you than reality. To put it in Myers-Briggs terms, you were 100% intuition and 0% sensory, and of course this was for a reason, and was not a cruel fate, but it did need to be lived out and thereby modified.

Now, seeing your life this way—using you though unknown as we have been using Hemingway *because* known—you can see that a person's actions, thoughts, reactions, may be as baffling to the person-group as to any others. What you do in life is not necessarily about what you think or assume or hope it is. There is so much going on behind the scenes. Is it a wonder that you sometimes awaken from a dream and wonder what you've been doing? But some people can live more comfortably knowing more, others, more comfortably knowing less. And—like the hired man Tarbox who said it to Emerson as a young man, that you like to quote occasionally—"people are always praying, and their prayers are always answered." You get out of life what the person-group really wants. The difficulty is that what the person-group wants and needs may be very different from what the volatile consciousness that is trying to coordinate the group (what you may call the ego) wants. That is the basis for much suffering, and in the largest sense all suffering is needless. However, that is a little too philosophical for life in the physical, we realize.

Nonetheless, let's say it again. In the sense that suffering is the difference between an ego's expectation or desire and a person-group's need and desire, all suffering is theoretically needless. *Does this not shed light on the virtues Christianity traditionally taught?* Patience, for instance? Faith? We teach nothing new, only suggesting a new way to see accustomed things not understood from the accustomed ways of seeing them. If instead of turning away from things that seem outdated or even repugnant, you see them as based on facts seen through another peephole, you can gain so much so quickly, because these other systems were worked out in detail, long ago.

I can't even remember the four cardinal virtues. Prudence and temperance were two, I think. Let me go look. [Looking in the

catechism that I bought a couple of years ago for just this purpose:]
fortitude, justice, prudence and temperance. I'll have to look up
what the catechism says about them, to see how it fits.

The key is *how* you look up elements of another systematic way of looking at life. If you are going to absorb the wisdom without becoming enmeshed in the system—and this is your goal here, of course—you need to temporarily enter into it, then retreat, reframe, and retain the insight, just as you did with the seven deadly sins.

If you were to look at the four cardinal virtues as your cheat-sheet to sneak you by the final exams so that you could get into heaven, they would be of no use to you whatever. It would be like trusting in the *ownership* of a roadmap to get you to your unknown destination, or more it would be like trusting that your *faith* in the roadmap would get you there. But that is absurd. The purpose of a roadmap is to represent relationships so that you will see which roads lead in which directions, and what you may expect to find along the way. Some don't need maps; some need them at first and not later; some always need them. But we can't think of any case in which somebody got to a destination by blind faith in the *concept* of a map.

GPS!

No, GPS is more like relying on guidance; it is a roadmap not spelled out but implicit.

The Limits to Intuition

Jim and Carol are friends of mine who communicate with you guys, sometimes through me but much more often directly, to see if they can help people. Recently they have been remote-viewing people's health conditions, much as Edgar Cayce did up to his death in 1945. Jim has devised an ingenious technique derived from dowsing practice. They get good and consistent answers (each dowsing separately, as a check on each other). The question is, why does the process sometimes not work. No, a better question is actually a set of questions:

—What are the limits on the process?
—What factors may interfere with it?
—Does the recipient's attitude affects the dowser's ability?
—What factors affect identifying the right person? Name alone? Address? Date of birth? Other things?

Plus, what else should we be asking you, but haven't thought to ask?

A good way to go about this, that set of questions. We can always ignore any or all specific questions if they don't go to the nub of it, but the phrasing of the questions focuses your mind.

Their approach is a nice corrective to Dr. McCoy of Star Trek, who trusted only to instruments and implements. Sensory function, you see. They *[Jim and Carol]* bring in the intuitive function, in order to make the sensory function *at first* less necessary, by pointing them in the right direction. But of course it would be unwise to rely on only one function. It would be the equivalent of Psychic's Disease. First get your intuitive diagnosis, then check to see if the diagnosis is accurate. Now, we recognize that this is not yet your question, but it is vital background for questions beyond medical techniques or dowsing techniques. In other words, it has much wider implications.

To employ intuitive and sensory functions each in the appropriate place and time, using each to support and backstop the other, is the correct use of human ability. This is entirely analogous to employing both thinking and feeling.

Dr. Jung? For, I heard you at the door, so to speak. [I don't know how to explain how certain different people have a different "feel," but they do, and often when they fade in or fade out, I am aware of the changing of the guard. And, of course, often enough not, too.]

Far more of medical practice is intuitive than is realized, in the same way and for the same reasons that your friend *[Ed Carter]* told you that the decisions made at the highest levels of corporations are always made on an intuitive basis: If they could be made on sensory data, they would be made earlier in the process. It is the function of intuition to supplement and sometimes supersede sensory data and reasoning dependent upon sensory data.

But clearly the use of intuition cannot safely be reduced to guesswork! Its proper use is as a light in the darkness, guiding you to the right place. But one does not operate on a patient by the illumination of lightning bolts, but by steady electrical lighting. An analogy, but—if you will pardon the pun—an illuminating one. Sudden certainty is the gift offered by intuition; careful checking of that certainty *[that is, the ability to check]* is the gift offered by the sensory routine.

But the specific question was, why do the dowsers sometimes get the wrong individuals, and how can this be avoided?

As so often happens, what seems a simple question actually contains within it many a complication.

If one is too close to the information received, for instance, it needlessly becomes entangled with peripheral or even irrelevant materials that "happen to be" present in the consciousness.

But on the theory that there are no accidents, how can that be a problem?

The "no accidents" mantra will not always serve you well, if misapplied. It is meant to indicate that nothing in the universe is by chance (despite appearances) and nothing is disconnected, as by nature it could not be. It is not meant to indicate that every causation is meaningful or significant.

I've heard that before, but where do you draw the line?[And about here Dr. Jung faded out and someone else, whom I have not identified beyond being "one of the guys," faded in.]

Accident and Necessity

Gurdjieff drew it—as you have never understood—by saying there was The Law of Necessity and The Law of Accident. We might paraphrase it by saying there is the law of what matters and the law of little things. Not every placement or relationship is meaningful. Who cares what you had for breakfast on the 13th of November—except in mystery novels, where little things become realized as significant things. No one can draw the line *ahead of time* between what is significant and what is not—nor, indeed, always after the fact. But the difference is there. (And of course what is significant to one may be not meaningful to the life of another.)

If we were to give you a rule of thumb, it would go somewhat like this. Those things closest to you polarize events most; those less important to you, less; those to which you are indifferent, not at all. But remember, everyone is in the same boat. So your fields produce cross-eddies.

Therefore there is chance in human affairs. Your everyday experience tells you that; your metaphysics denies it. Here is how to tie the two. No important event in your life—no important thought—no important person—no important decision—occurs by chance. They respond to what you are; they result from what you are. And if life were only one timeline, your lives could be said to be predetermined, for obviously anything stemming from what you already are is in that sense predestined, each "inevitable" event being built upon what preceded it. It is only in that you move by changing timelines that you exercise the free choice that is—as we have told you many times—the point of your existence. But which leaf falls on which side of the fence does not matter, and so falls under Gurdjieff's Law of Accident—unless it *does* matter, in which case it falls under the Law of Necessity. A moment's thought should show you that what is under the one law in one timeline may be under the other in another. Same person, same event or decision or whatever, but a different relationship because other things are different.

Now, to dowsing. Suppose you are to find Joe Smith. Do you need his date of birth, or social security number, or ZIP code, or what? Do you need only the clear intent to connect with him? (And why should you need more? It is mind to mind, is it not?) The answer lies in the difference between The Law Of Necessity and The Law Of Accident. Can you guess how?

No. I do think that a prospective psychic diagnosis—a dowsing of conditions—would fall under The Law of Necessity always, if by that you mean something of importance to the individual.

Ah, but *does* it? Think for instance of how many people go to fortune-tellers, they know not quite why, and therefore hear predictions they don't really put any stock in, yet do not forget. Some come true, some don't. What is going on there?

I suppose, insufficient desire leads to lack of polarization? But what if it's a bad medium or an outright fraud?

If the polarization is strong, do you suppose you would be led to a bad or fraudulent medium?

Then—in the case of dowsing—is the intent of the dowsers not enough?

Clearly not, or anyone could know everything and anything.

Then what is the variable? The intent of the person asking? The intent of an intermediary?

Variables—vary. It could be external circumstances, or the viewer, or the recipient's mind, or anything or nothing—*if* the polarization is absent. If not absent, nothing can interfere. It boils down to this: Nothing and no one is infallible, and this is by the design of things, the way things are and must be.

You don't get that either. Let's try again. If an event is a conjunction of a significant number of timelines, is increasingly under The Law of Necessity. That is a tautology, in fact. But if the coin comes down sometimes heads, sometimes tails, which timeline you take determines which you will perceive, and the less determined it is, the less it is a part of The Law of Necessity. Again, a tautology. How are you to distinguish ahead of time what you are dealing with? You can't. You can only do your best and see what happens and then deal with that.

So, if the dowsers get a request, they can't know ahead of time that their best efforts are going to tell them the situation. The better they are and the purer their intent and the more they are attuned, the better they'll do, but any given reading may be wrong for reasons way outside of their control?

Does this not agree with your experience of life?

Yeah, it does. It's the same way with doing this. No guarantees and check your work.

That's not so impossible a set of ground rules to follow, is it?

In practice, no. So, to sum up—do their best, don't look for a magic formula that would convey infallibility because it doesn't exist, and check everything derived by intuition, using whatever sensory checks are available.

Yes. Well received.

Our Situation as Individuals

The situation you begin from is as it is because it proceeds from your past. Even if it is a condition at birth, it may be considered to proceed from the past in that it is the result of what was chosen for the body in the shaping of the ring. That is, the combination of elements, and the mating of the elements to a specific genetic heritage, set the boundaries, and within them were certain conditions established.

Always—wherever and whenever you are, it is here and now. Always your free will exerts itself on the results of past decisions. Where else could you begin but from where you find yourself?

Your various constituent parts have made their peace with that past, or perhaps we should say, they have each fitted into the pattern, even when their manner of fitting in has been to fit in *at odds with* the rest of it, or a large part of it. It is no surprise, is it, that a pattern should contain contradictory parts?

In short, any starting-place is the result of past maneuverings and accommodations and warfare—and every conceivable nuance of relationship. What you are is what you have decided to be, one way or another. You may have decided to settle for something, out of weariness or lack of vision or lack of knowledge or lack of consciousness, but for whatever reason, any given moment may be considered to be a moment of rest. It is your previous landing-pad, and your present launching-pad. Always.

So perhaps in that context it is clearer that you *decide* to change before you change; you do not change as a result of external forces. *External* forces do not and can not exist.

Think about that.

In all aspects of your life, not just health, *external forces do not exist.* There is no external, for the inner and outer are one. *This is not empty rhetoric.* This is a plain statement of truth. You cannot be the victim of forces that do not exist.

But then—you will be tempted to ask—how is it that our everyday experience convinces us that external forces not only *do* exist but exist in an overpowering strength? You all know the answer even when you repeat loudly that you *don't* know it. It's the same old question of definition. Who is "you"? Who is "I"?

The ringmaster may or may not know. It is the ringmaster's task in life, perhaps, to bring his constituent elements into a harmonious knowledge of the fact that there is no external. But regardless of the extent of the ringmaster's knowledge, or of the internal diversity the ringmaster contends with (and draws strength from), the *self* knows, and will pass that knowing along whenever the ringmaster does not block it.

Our intuition can tell us, when we once reach a certain state of coherence.

That is, your intuition can tell you *in such a way as to be heard,* once you cease to block the message for one reason or another. External forces do not exist. Pretty important statement.

Humility and Gratitude

All right, my friends. It is all coming together nicely—which I suppose should be an indicator that it's about to be pulled to pieces, or blown to bits.

Would we do that to you? We smile.

You mean, would you do that to us—again. But I'm certainly not complaining! I thought yesterday's material was just wonderful and again I thank you for it and for this whole series. I joke with you—and about you—a lot, but you know how greatly privileged I feel to be in such a connection.

As well you should—to use your own joke. But—seriously meant, too. The connection is available to all; it's just a matter of desire and application. But not everyone will or should live their lives as you live yours, and not anyone will or should experience just what you are experiencing, any more than you can live anyone else's life, or would enjoy it if you could. So—it is always well to understand the particular ways in which your individual lives have been blessed, and to be grateful for it. Far better be grateful than to confuse blessings bestowed with rights earned! In other words, with thanks goes humility. And humility is always a productive state of mind, far more than any sense of entitlement or any sense of appropriation of credit for gifts.

Chapter Five

Shaping Your Life

"The relatively few who will use the key [Jung's key to the unconscious] will so gain in the weight and authoritativeness of personality which comes from being all-of-a-piece that they may become the grain of mustard-seed or the leaven which leavens the whole lump."
—*Jung's Contribution to Our Time*, by Eleanor Bertine, Page 29

"What are your sources of satisfaction? If they are meats and drinks, dress, gossip, revenge, hope of wealth, they must perish with the body. If they are contemplation, kind affections, admiration of what is admirable, self-command, self-improvement, then they survive death and will make you as happy then as now."
—R.W. Emerson, December 1831

It isn't enough to *see* your life differently. You must *live* your best understanding, or new ideas will only add confusion. Understanding is incomplete until you live it day to day. And what good are ideas as playthings, if we need anchors for our lives? Let's begin by summing up the description of life that we have gotten from the guys upstairs, individually by name or anonymously.

- Everything is alive and conscious.

- Everything is *connected.*

- This physical world rests upon and emerges from a non-physical world with different rules.

- Time and space produce separation and delayed consequences, and allow disparate elements to mix in a way they cannot easily mix in the non-physical.

- Physical life is for shaping new minds—new souls. After our physical deaths, the mind (the soul) that was shaped is what its choices in life have made it.

The purpose of life is implicit in these few statements.

Every age has its characteristic way of thinking, and any new model must rest on new definitions. This model defines us not as economic units, or social units but as individuals who aren't nearly as individual as we think ourselves. Convenient fiction, the guys call the concept of the individual. Habit-patterns, they call our minds.

Us they describe as being a sort of group of threads held together in a ring, with our developed and developing consciousness as the ringmaster. They think of us as comprising three levels: the person-mind, our personality; strand-minds, which are the traits that are part of us, whether expressed or not, and group-mind, the higher-level minds to which we are as strands. Our task in life is to manage that group—to fuse it into one coordinated mind—so that it can continue to operate in the absence of the body. That is the point of life, to forge a soul.

Throughout our physical life, we remain connected to the non-physical world. It is an extension of ourselves, the non-part of our physical being. And it is our resonance with various other disembodied intelligences. If we are connected to these either through our physical heredity or through resonance, or both, we have the potential to interact with them. Such interaction offers us the chance to live more fulfilling lives, because it offers us access to a source of wisdom that is willing—anxious, even—to assist us to get what we want. But communication is a matter of choice. We may choose to remain closed, or may choose to open up a little bit, or may choose to open wide. It's all the same to them, or rather, whatever their preference, they absolutely respect our right to decide.

This model opens up two lines of self-development: (1) greater access to guidance, and (2) the pursuit of wholeness, which implies greater freedom from unconscious behaviors. The latter part of this chapter offers simple techniques to help you to maximize your health and consciously develop specific qualities using visualizations, to establish better connection with non-physical guidance, and to reprogram unwanted repetitive behaviors. First, though, more from the guys—named and unnamed—on shaping our lives.

Ships

There is a large number of what we might term the intelligent unanchored, of which you are one. We do *not* mean ungrounded, for the ungrounded cannot do the work we refer to here. You are unanchored in that you have no body of authority that you recognize as absolute or even as compelling. Indeed, you are so made that you actively resist the idea that there could be such an authority. It amounts to a resistance to codes. The only authority you will accept is what publishes itself to you personally, just like Henry Thoreau, and even more than Emerson.

I see that. I scarcely read a chapter of Walden and I was Thoreau's man emotionally and intellectually and spiritually, though I wouldn't have used that word. That was 40 years ago this coming fall [that is, in 1970], and nothing has changed about that instinctive acceptance, indeed delight, this although years go by in which I do not read his words. He became part of me, or probably I should say he activated part of me which I forever associate with his person and mind.

Thoreau was unanchored, you see. So was Hemingway. So was Lincoln. You will scarcely find a major influence in your life who had a central authority and clung to it. Thus Thomas Merton, for all the instinctive sympathy you feel for his honest explorations, remains quite a secondary figure, not part of your personal pantheon, precisely (though you have thought for other reasons) because he willingly and *by his nature* accepted the authority of Holy Mother the Church. It isn't that he was born to it—like Hemingway he was a convert—but that his nature required a spiritual anchor, as his previous rootless unsatisfying life demonstrated to him.

Oddly, Chesterton, too, I suppose. I hadn't thought of him in this way until now, but suddenly it is obvious, and I can see why he too converted to Catholicism, despite its deep unpopularity in the English society he flourished in.

Yes. He had an instinctive anchor, and in time he found its external correlate. There's a reason for churches, after all: Certain types require them, and it isn't merely what you call sheep-itude. GK Chesterton wasn't exactly a sheep, nor was Thomas Merton. However, they are not you, and their needs and opportunities are not yours. You and your friends and your fellow unanchored friends known and unknown to you require something different, for you are not unanchored—as Chesterton and Merton were—only because you have not found your anchor. You are unanchored because you are *sailing*.

You've said the like before: Ships are safe in the harbor but that's not what ships are for.

Well, more than that. Ships are meant to anchor safely at the end of any voyage. Anchoring safely is not a sign of defeat or of lack of enterprise, but only an external sign of what stage of its life that particular ship happens to be in. It is no particular virtue, no particular vice, to exist at anchor or with anchors hoisted. Everything depends upon your stage in life, so to speak.

But you want me to speak primarily to those whose anchors are up, or who can find no anchorage.

Who else would listen? Who else would you know from experience how to speak to? Who else could profitably hear what message you have to pass along?

So—to return before we lose sight of it—a gradual transfer of the initiative?

Surely it is implied in what we have been saying. You and those who resemble you cannot follow; therefore you must have been shaped to lead, or to go your own way. If you are to do so safely, productively, you need to assure a proper reliable connection to what you call Guidance.

Living Close to the Unconscious

Dr. Jung, I just read, in Memories, Dreams, Reflections, *your statement how hard it is for most people to live close to the unconscious. Is that what I am doing, or do you mean something different?*

Well, you know, one means different things depending on who is reading, and when in his life one reads it! At this time in your life it is open to you in a way that it was not, just a short time ago.

To live in close proximity—on neighborly terms, let us say—to the unconscious is to be very clear, very transparent, to the promptings of the spirit. It means, to not allow the conscious mind—the ego-bound mind—to tyrannize over the entire being, as if only it were the arbiter, the judge, and only its needs were to be considered and fulfilled. The conscious self, unbalanced by knowledge of the unconscious, easily comes to think itself the only thing in the world. You think "autistic" and although this is somewhat extravagant it is not without suggestive value.

To live on good terms with the unconscious is to live in the perpetual awareness of not being the center even of your own world, let alone the other world! And this people fear. Their external life already leaves them feeling insufficient and unnecessary. To add to that the feeling that internally, too, one is only a hanger-on, a bit player rather than the starring role, may be too much to bear. In reality of course it is not that the conscious self, the ego self, is at all unnecessary. Without the ego self the soul would have no locus! Yet it may appear to the unprepared just that way.

You yourself live much less often on good terms with the surrounding unconscious than you sometimes believe, for often enough you close your access—as is your right—and find yourself isolated, directionless and depressed. This is the inevitable result of cutting oneself off from the mainsprings of one's being. Yet, other times you do lead a more symbolic, undefined life in connection with you know not what. I would say that you do this working from an instinct that leads you to do much as I did in the tower, reducing the din of your contemporaries as your friend Henry Thoreau also did. This is a good thing to do, if not done in imitation because someone did it but because they sparked you with an idea which itself inspired you. Thus, building fires answers a need in you, and so heating your little *[wood-stove-heated]* house was a comfort and a quiet joy, rather than work as others would have found it. No TV, no radio except at odd moments, also reduces the distractions of the immediate moment. You must watch your appetite for the internet lest it overpower your central solitude but it does serve as a corrective, for you still need connection. In this, though, you are acting as intermediary rather than consumer, and this too is better. Caesar never read a newspaper—but if they had existed, would have. Napoleon read newspapers and would have listened to radio. Mussolini listened to radio and would have monitored television. It is balance, not any particular detail or prohibition, that is the goal.

Wholeness

As we pointed out in connection with Hemingway—*wholeness attracts*. It is its own initial credential, which is then backed up or not backed up by specific knowledge. But plenty of people have knowledge and cannot express it or even tap into it, necessarily, due to self-division that prevents who and what they are from coalescing into a powerful unity. To put it another way, when your person-group elements all pull together, you get fabulous results that cannot be obtained when half of them are fighting the other half. That's one benefit of doing the work on yourself. You have been doing the work on yourself not, primarily, by doing this writing but by remaining open to input and being helpful and open to others. Many of those who read this have seen similar results from similar efforts but may not have drawn the conclusions.

Do you want to change the world? There are many external paths, all the way from the hermit to the warrior to the activist to the propagandist—any external role you can imagine. But there is only *one* internal path to effectiveness, and that is internal cohesion. Is it not obvious that no self-divided person can be as effective as that same person with all its active constituent groups acting in concert?

Yes, I can feel you entering. Dr. Jung?

One begins with the concept of the individual being not so much an individual but a *potential* individual, a community wanting to be made into a coherent whole. Is not my work associated with the word individuation? Your experience here, and the concepts you have been given over a ten-year span, allow you to see the term and the process and the desired end-result in a different light. Begin with the concept of a person-group— a grouping within one body (so to speak) of many traits and inheritance that *may* learn to function as a unit or may not. Does this not make the nature of the task and opportunity of life clearer? You did not well understand the concept of crystallizing the self when it was presented to you in the sessions that became your book [*The Sphere and the Hologram*], but this is what they amounted to. And if you will go back and look at the sessions that referenced the concept, you will see that your potential comprehension was seriously handicapped by the fact that you lacked certain underlying concepts that would have made things clearer.

Life amid Polarities

[I realized one day that I wanted greater continuity of purpose. Immediately, I heard: "So change your control panel." (I think of it as a tool to visualize priorities and emphasize or de-emphasize them by moving a slide-switch. I describe how to create and use one later in the chapter.) I started to do so, and came to a difficulty.]

It would seem, though, that the quality of continuity must have its opposite, not merely its absence. Gentlemen, a more accurate description of these slide-switches, please?

They aren't exactly opposites nor even, quite, polarities. It is more like opposing tendencies. That after all is the nature of spirals, though you may never have thought of it: love and fear; expansion and contraction, spiraling out and spiraling in. At every point along the continuity, the balance between continuing in that direction and reversing course is slightly different. There wouldn't be much complexity, much potential, if as you moved in one direction you met only increased resistance, or, alternatively, if as you progressed increased inertia assisted you to continue. In either system you would soon find and pass a point of no return—the first would tend to settle you in the middle between extremes; the second would tend to have you accelerate to one or the other extreme. Neither arrangement would maximize your play of free will *at any given moment,* which is how and why the system is set up.

At either extreme a spiral might almost be represented as a sine wave—up and down and forward, up and down and forward, pretty regular, pretty symmetrical. The carrier wave progresses in one direction, by alternating between poles at right angles to that direction. But in the middle it is as if the sine wave becomes deformed from a 90 degree angle to the direction of flow to a 45 degree angle. It is in a sense as if the wave "wanted to" go toward the end the wave is traveling toward—*seen either way.*

Draw a coil and imagine the coil suspended in space between two forces, say a positive and negative charge. Don't worry about the analogy too much, just get an image. Each opposing charge pulls on the spiral. It should be clear that any point on the spiral is either exactly equidistant between the two forces, or closer to one or to the other. So there can be only three states relative to the forces: plus, zero, or minus.

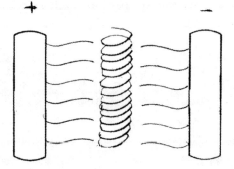

Note that for the purposes of this illustration, plus and minus have nothing to do with good and evil, or helpful and obstructive, or any such polarity. They may be between, say, line and shape, or texture and weight. In other words, we are here showing a mechanical understanding (in analogy, again we remind you) *not* a disguised moral lesson.

Well, the oscillation back and forth between polarities is regular, predictable, and useful in subjecting you to ever-varying influences within which to exercise your will. Some times will be extremely favorable to some purposes, extremely unfavorable for others. Other times will be more or less indifferent—*as seen in the context of any one issue.* Your whole life doesn't revolve around one spiral, or again where would free will be? Instead you have spirals within spirals, some contradicting others, some in harmonic resonance with others, some not interacting with others in any system that is obvious to you. Thus we might say that every moment of your life is uniquely favorable for something; and more or less favorable for other things, and indifferent for still other things, and so to the other pole.

If you were to draw a stretched-out spiral and indicate that from any point on that spiral other spirals emanated, and others from them, you *might* begin to get a sense of the complexity of life *and* the underlying rhythms of it. Hence astrology, numerology and other such systems: Hints may certainly be obtained as to structure and operation. In actual life, so many spirals are simultaneously operating that the underlying clockwork is hard to detect. It may be felt; seen through the side of the eye, so to speak.

Now we need to leave the question of the oscillation for a moment and remember that we are concerned with direction along the length of the spiral. If we were to assume, as you on your side all too often *do* assume—that the purpose of life is to "get somewhere," to reach the end of the process, to get beyond dualities and polarities, then clearly you might say the spiral motion is just unneeded distraction on your way to proceeding from one end of the spiral to another. Looked at that way, a spiral is an inefficient way to proceed from minus to plus, because of all the extra material involved in making the coils!

But maybe life is not about going from one end of a coil to another. Maybe life is about being suspended between forces in any given plane, and at the same time between forces in another plane, and another, and another—with the net effect that you are balanced among so many forces that *your will* determines where you will go and what you experience. Those who (laughably) use their free will to assume an intellectual position denying free will have let themselves be deluded by mechanical rather than electrical analogies, and by simple rather than complex models. Imagine yourself not only suspended between poles in any one plane but in *all* planes and you will have a better idea of your situation.

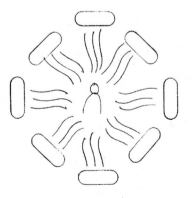

Now—we know this can be difficult but we're trying to help—put these two analogies together as best you can. Do *not* think of yourself as being joined to a metal spiral, forced merely to follow its curve as it goes. And yet—in a way that is true. Do *not* think of yourself as infinitely free at any moment to do, feel, be whatever you please. And yet—in a way that is true. As always, the truth lies between opposites, and includes them, and transcends them. Life is never as simple as models of life. Yet it is not something that cannot be grasped, only the grasping of life is done by *living* it.

Life is cycles, and that is the determined part of your lives. But it is of so many cycles—as we say, some obviously inter-related, some not, that the net effect is freedom. And that is by design, for if man were not free to choose, we on this side would get no benefit from 3D Theater. It is your choosing that stirs the pot, as you like to say. Human activity—and all activity is choice—is the random factor that provides life to the system. Oh, you could say (rightly) "not random because the result of causes that might conceivably be mapped"—but this would be a sterile correctness. What *good* does it do you, to cling to the idea that freedom is illusion? It is illusion *from one way of seeing*, but not from others—and that way of seeing does not empower, it does exactly the opposite. And what is worse, it is no more correct than saying "random because the number of ultimate causes is great enough that the net effect is incalculable and may be overridden." It is all in Swedenborg.

That's a long ride, and I thank you for it. So what is the opposite value to continuity?

We smile. You had enough continuity to go back several pages to retrieve the question. What is your answer.

System, then?

Reminders. You want to live in the moment, remembering, and anticipating. Thus—stretch the moment, stretch your effective consciousness, and you will have what you need.

Awareness of now. Awareness of then. Hard to envision a slide-switch for it.

Don't postulate an opposition that postulates choice and exclusion. Try "awareness of here and now" at one end, "extended awareness" at the other end, and move the slide where you want it.

Discouragement, Its Causes and Cure

Is [my brother] Paul entirely right, that discouragement is built of "falsely conceived expectations of ourselves"?

It isn't like he is immune to discouragement. No one is, it is a human characteristic, and perhaps we shall say something about it.

Life, you know, is about getting back up again after you have fallen or been pushed (same thing, really, when you look at it clearly enough). Those who "succeed" are those who refuse to stay down. They get up one time more than they fall, someone said. (Do you *know* how much stuff like that you have crammed in here? We smile.) But when you look at life in the way we have been encouraging you to do, what do you find? All choices are made, hence any choice is fine, in and of itself. You're not going to ruin the world or even your life—a choice is merely a choice among versions of your life to stroll down. Sort of.

Outside of time and space, where we can see the pattern of the *whole* worm rather than only one transverse segment at a time—how should we be discouraged? In a way (*only* "in a way") we can't even take it, or any mood, very seriously. We take them *as* seriously as, but no *more* seriously than, any other part of your life.

Every present moment in your life is exaggerated.

Let's say that again for emphasis. From a perspective outside time-space, you live every present moment as if it were your life rather than just one moment in your life. Necessarily, each moment comes to you in exaggerated size, importance, impact. Nothing wrong with this, and we *certainly* are *not* saying "don't live in the moment." You *should!* You *must!* You *do!* But—

Recognize that any given moment is unlike all the rest of your life in that its immediacy is total, its intensity is therefore exaggerated (sometimes to the point of leaving you feeling trapped), and—all of these by definition—it is *fleeting*. All your past, all your future—including the past when you began this sentence and the future when you end it, not very long, but both quite clearly not "now" (which just moved again)—every moment of your life *except for one* share (seemingly) the characteristics of *non*-immediacy, *non*-intensity (we'll talk about this; it is language getting in the way), and *non*-fleeting-ness.

When you can see it that way—the immediate fleeting moment that you spend your life riding like a surfer on a wave, and *all other moments* on the other hand—doesn't that look a little different from the old "past present future" model? As we say, your immediate moment always by definition is out of scale, because it seems to you to be realer than the rest of your life—and this, regardless whether you are living in daydreams of past or future, for you are always daydreaming, by definition, *now!*

Well, if you accept that the present moment always and necessarily appears different to you than any other moment of your life—and we cannot see that the point can be argued—then what of discouragement?

Do you know what discouragement is, really, in our perspective? It is a sort of failure of belief, almost a failure of nerve, certainly a failure of vision, usually caused by an interruption in the connection Upstairs, as you say. *This is not meant as a chastisement.* Not for you, not for anyone who reads this. Chastisements ought to be reserved for those who willingly and consciously choose to do what they know they should not do. Therefore, this does not apply. (Indeed—not to stray too far from the subject in hand—chastisement is rarely effective, hence rarely warranted. It assumes more self-knowledge than usually exists, either in the chastisee or chastiser! Enough lest we sidetrack ourselves.)

Failure of belief. Failure of nerve. Failure of vision. Failure of (or anyway interference with) connection. What do we mean by this?

Failure of *belief* means forgetting what at other times you know or at least strongly believe, that "they're not going to lead me out into the wilderness and leave me there," that your life can be trusted. Failure of *nerve* means that you are taking counsel of your fears. Failure of *vision* means you are wavering in your aims, fearing that they cannot be realized. Failure of *connection* merely means you are accidentally or willfully "going it alone" without using the greater resources available to you.

None of these are *moral* failings, more like compass deviation.

And for those of us who are prone to discouragement?

Stop discouraging yourself. Really, just stop. That is, set into motion an automatic counter-force. When you find yourself getting discouraged (and you will, everyone does, it cannot well be avoided) have an *automatic* response, so that it comes into play without your having to make a particular effort to engage it—for when you are discouraged, almost any effort will seem greater than it is worth.

So for instance, if you get discouraged you might have an image that you can recall. Not an exhortation, *not* self-chiding. An image. An attractive image, a symbol, representing something where your heart is. It could be the aerial photo of the Island of Iona, for you. It could be a mental picture of Henry Thoreau at

Walden. It could be any image of those you love, best combined somehow with an image symbolizing your continuing aspirations. The purpose of the symbol, of the image, is to reconnect you emotionally—that is all you need or ever will need.

If discouragement is a failure of nerve, vision, belief, connection—no *logic*, no *thought*, no *will-power* can correct this. But a heart-connected image can. Once the thread is back in your consciousness, then it is a decision for you—"will I choose to continue to be depressed, or will I get back on the invisible path I sleepwalk so well?" *As* a choice, this represents your freedom, you see, for you *might* and perhaps sometimes *will* choose to wallow in discouragement for a while—but you can, if you wish, emerge without doing so, merely because the image lets you reconnect without having to summon energies for a special effort.

A magical tool, if you will. And this (not to beat the subject to death) is another example of things the Christians knew that could profitably be more widely disseminated in your day among the unchurched.

Anyone who led an aspiring life has had to face moments of discouragement, and of course similar tools and techniques evolve regardless of differences of times and cultures. For one thing, there is the connection with us. We are the spiders in the center of the web of days, so to speak!

How refreshing to see you finally use an unflattering analogy for yourselves instead of us!

Not a bad analogy, actually, except for the overtone of prey. Spiders are endlessly patient, waiting for something to hit the web; they are endlessly industrious (remember the story about Robert the Bruce), persevering forever; they are at the center of a web spun from themselves. And perhaps we don't think of them as ugly or frightful.

Well, worms and spiders are not natural enemies, that's good. Thanks for all this—not only for the sake of the material that I will put out on the web (if you'll pardon the expression) but for what sounds to be a very useful tool. And—as always—for the connection itself, the breath of life to me.

Awakening

[The Buddha said—I am awake. Awakening is not difficult, but it requires intent and vigilance, and it's easier with partners, if you make certain agreements between yourselves. Gurdjieff talked of sleep and how no work can be done in sleep. So how do we wake up? First, we need to see that what we are mostly doing right now is going through life asleep, mostly on automatic pilot, with any given stimulus meeting an automatic response or generating an automatic association of ideas and reactions. Two kinds of screens shield us from the world: one is like a screensaver, fast-moving, blurring the world behind it, the other is like wallpaper, persisting and forcing us to guess what is behind it. Our job is to stop the blur and put aside the screen. What is behind them is reality. It's that simple conceptually. The difficult thing is learning how to do it, and then remembering to do it]

Time to change the metaphor?

Time anyway to do more thinking about the subject—that is, to recalibrate consciousness, which in a way is what thinking *is*, or to reprogram yourself (as we shall explain) which is also what thinking is, except that this is a particular kind of thinking done in a particular way. In all this, you're going to have to realize that you are not reinventing the wheel. *Are* not, *should* not, and in any case *could* not. An attempt to do so would be futile and misleading and ultimately discouraging to anyone who tried to follow that new truth. Consider all scientific and religious and metaphysical thought as a resource, not an obstacle. Think of them as containers of symbols that you can unpack and then re-pack, with a great gain in processing power.

I hear you intending to say that we can come to a much more sophisticated and powerful understanding of what you are telling us if we will look into the accumulated wisdom of various disciplines to find examples of what they know that we can profitably reinterpret in light of this material, and so come to the same material from more than one viewpoint, in more than one context.

It seems to us that this is just what we said. Very well. Now let us move away from the analogy of robots. Just as we first used strings-and-rings, as you call it, in order to loosen previous concepts, and are now humanizing the concept by referring to person-groups, so we used robots to loosen your connection to automatic behavior and will proceed to humanize the concept by tying it in to other things.

You will bear in mind that we said you deal with three layers of being at once, a larger group of which you are but a thread, your own group that you often think of as "I" and the smaller groups each of which you experience as one thread in your own group. (This disregards the fact that you may at times see more than one layer up or down the chain, and also may sometimes hold in consciousness both the layer above and that below. Such experiences happen, but for the moment we disregard them for the sake of conceptual clarity and simplicity.)

The other thing that you will have to remember is that "up" and "down" are spatial analogies. (For that matter, so are "inner" and "outer.") There is no practical way to discard their usage and still say anything meaningful, but bear in mind that a thing may be both "bigger than you" and "smaller than you" at the same time. In fact, it may be at the same time bigger, smaller, and the same. There is no way to cram that fact into a spatial analogy, but it is no less true.

Three Simple Techniques

I omit the brackets, but the rest of this chapter is not the guys, but me. As promised, here are simple techniques to help you to reprogram unwanted repetitive behaviors, to establish better connection with non-physical guidance, and to maximize your health and consciously develop specific qualities using visualizations, followed by suggestions on how to remember to stay connected.

1. Reprogramming

You know how frustrating life can be. Time after time, we do what we don't want to do, and don't do what we do want to do. We defeat our own purposes, and don't know why. Our lives may be filled with accidents or diseases. We may suffer physical or emotional injuries that continue to affect us for years, even decades. We may wrestle with depression, and anger, or may find ourselves feeling spiritually devastated, internally empty and dead, forcing ourselves to go on, day by meaningless and painful day.

These problems, which so often seem to have no solution, are actually *external* manifestations of your *internal* condition. There are no accidents. You are who you are, where you are, for a reason. Start where you are. (You have no choice, but it's good to know that you're in the right place at the right time.) Since external events always illuminate our inner world, it's really true that every problem is an opportunity. And, the more stubborn the problem, the greater the potential for growth. There are no accidents, no tragedies, no victims, villains, or innocent bystanders. Therefore, it makes no sense to blame others (which puts us into helpless victimhood), or make excuses, (which provides story to keep us stuck), or explain things away as "chance" (which denies our own responsibility).

The key to a fuller, richer life is achieving a greater, richer, more fluid consciousness, and you can do it. It's just a matter of learning how. You can overcome past traumas, and integrate forgotten sources of unproductive attitudes and resistances. That's easy to say, I know, but it's also surprisingly easy to do. The answer to all your problems can be found by looking carefully at various internal mechanisms that have been programmed to respond automatically whenever external life presses a button. Following Colin Wilson, I used to call these automatic mechanisms robots. We use them every day. They drive our cars, they tie our shoes, they remember how to read and write. You could almost define learning as the process of splitting off a piece of your consciousness to perform some task automatically for you.

These mechanisms are necessary and useful But sometimes, they function in ways that work to our disadvantage. It may be that the situation for which they were created has changed. Or they have the wrong idea about what we want and how to get it. Or they may be functioning exactly as designed, but you've changed your mind about what you want. The problem is, they are *unconscious!* They can't reprogram themselves. If they're going to be reprogrammed, you're going to have to be the one to do it. (Their state of consciousness appears to be dream-like, with no awareness of a changing present. Each "robot," I think, is actually a snapshot of a time in our life when some problem became embodied. Nothing has changed since the last time it shared consciousness, and it can't change on its own.)

What I used to call robots now seem to me more like executable computer files. When they were written, they began to execute the instructions they were given. Unless and until they are reprogrammed, they will continue to do so. And how do we reprogram them? We simply call them into consciousness—in our analogy, we bring them into active RAM—change them, and resave them. In other words, the only thing necessary is to contact them and inform them of what you want.

Sound too good to be true? It isn't. All we need to do, to reshape our lives, is to identify old behaviors that no longer serve us, call them into active consciousness (which means *feeling* the circumstances that gave birth to them, not merely thinking about them) and update their instructions. The art of reprogramming these old patterns is the secret of self-transformation. That is not exaggeration.

This involves three steps.

One, get into the *feeling* you were in when you did the original programming. Whenever you find yourself acting automatically, in a way you wish to change, identify the feeling that accompanies that behavior. I don't mean "label" the feeling, I mean become consciously aware of it. You must be in the feeling to contact the robot. Otherwise, it's just words and can have no effect. Once you are sure that you are in the feeling, ask where the feeling came from. "How are you serving me?" Remaining in the feeling, ask, "what is the origin of this?" Wait for an answer. It could be a memory, a thought, a visual, words, pictures. Wait for an answer. When something surfaces, go with it. Don't demand impossible certainty.

Two, do the *analysis* to find out what caused the programming. Ask how the origin led to the condition. "How did being yelled at unexpectedly as a small child lead to an inability to deal with people's anger?" Some will find analysis easier than getting into the feelings, others will find it harder. But both steps are necessary. Ask, "how are you serving me by presenting me with this situation?" *Not* as accusation or rhetoric! Expect to be told. Receive, being alert, determined, and non-judgmental. Analyze the connection between what started it and how it manifests. Interact with that part of your consciousness

Three, *reprogram* to meet your current needs. Send acceptance and love: "Thank you for serving me." Provide clear instructions "I don't want you to do A any more. Until further notice, do B." Listen to any arguments it may have and reassure it. Reprogram it according to what you want. Then, "Thank you for serving me now and in the past."

This can be done whenever you discover unconscious behaviors you wish to change.

2. Guidance

Getting in touch with guidance is another of those things that is easier done than said. We extend beyond time/space, and it's easy to get information from the part of ourselves that is in the non-physical, and it's easy for that part to get information from others on that side of the veil. This technique is easily learned and easily practiced, and I have taught the basics to a roomful of people in three hours. First we perceive: We act as if we were positive, though we don't have any objective data. Then we interpret, using our rational skills. You must receive first (or you have nothing to judge), but you must judge at some point (or you may become a flake).

Fortunately, *you don't need to know what you're doing*. In my experience, stumbling along works just fine. Intent, and perseverance, more than any other qualities, will get you where you want to go. Trust your inner knowing; it will bring you farther, surer, than conscious knowledge.

However, *you can't be certain*. You may accumulate evidence, and you may perhaps convince yourself and perhaps others beyond a reasonable doubt. But how are you to *prove* anything? In the final analysis, we believe a thing because it resonates with something within us—or we don't because it doesn't. In psychic matters, get used to acting and believing *provisionally*, trusting your best judgment but remembering that you may be wrong. Just because you're dealing with the other side doesn't mean that you can safely assume that you (or they) are infallible.

Don't expect to be able to predict. The guys upstairs, in other material, say that all potential pasts, presents and futures exist, and we move among them, consciously or otherwise. Any prediction may prove to be "wrong" merely because we move not to the future foreseen but to some alternative. This being so, what is the point in making predictions?

Finally, this is *a skill, to be learned like any other.* Could you ride a bicycle flawlessly the first time you got onto one? Could you speak a foreign language fluently after one lesson? Tuning in to the other side is an innate human ability, but as in most things in life, improvement comes only with practice.

Here's how you do it. Think of a question you really would like the answer to. (However, don't ask life-or-death questions, or try to predict the future. You don't want your anxiety to choke off access.) Set your intention to contact only those beings who have your highest good at heart. Don't worry if you think you can't do it. There's no harm in trying.

Keep your ego out of it. Don't keep score. And don't succumb to the illusion of distance: There isn't any obstacles to overcome, no wall to climb. We are all connected. Don't worry, at first, about whether what you get is true. And don't worry about who the source is, any more than you worry about the source of your dreams. The question is, does the information resonate? Is it helpful? Avoid excess caution. (You don't have to be sure.) Avoid censoring yourself. (The information doesn't have to make sense immediately.) Just assume that it can be done. It may feel like you are pretending. Allow that feeling. In fact, go ahead and pretend if it's necessary to get started. (Often it is necessary.) Don't fall into Psychic's Disease, thinking that if you feel it strongly, it must be true, and don't fall into the opposite error of thinking that if you don't have a logical explanation, what you're feeling or what you perceived must be false.

Ask the question, then *wait* for an answer! Don't press, don't make it up to avoid having nothing to say. Input may come in many forms: images, ideas, words, lyrics, association, memory. Or you may just get a knowing, or a hunch. Sometimes you get just cloudy, vague impressions, and maybe none of it immediately makes sense. But while you're reporting, remember three don'ts: Don't judge. Don't guess. Don't use logic. This process isn't like collecting data. It's closer to empathy. In the initial stage, that of perception, *thinking* is not only useless, but detrimental. *Analysis* is totally the wrong track. Only *empathy* destroys the illusion of separation, the illusion of distance between us. Think of a mother with her newborn, for instance. Jot down whatever wells up, in whatever form it takes. Jot words as keys for you to remember. You're not after a polished production. The sequence is, first perceive, then judge. But *perceive* during the exercise, don't *judge* until later! Then, use your discernment to judge what you have received. It's new data; weigh it.

3. Visualizations

You can maximize your access to health by the use of two or three simple but powerful visualization techniques.

1) *The "River Of Life And Health" meditation.* This one is first and foremost. If you don't do anything else, do this one. It is powerful and cannot possibly hurt anyone, ever.

Get into a comfortable sitting position and close your eyes. Take a few slow deep breaths, briefly holding your breath after you breathe in, and again after you breathe out. Relax. Imagine yourself standing under a waterfall, with the river of life and health flowing around you and through you. These waters represent our invisible support from the other side. They flow through us day and night, or we could not live, but mostly we live unaware of this silent unfailing support. The waters flow *through* you, penetrating every cell. See the waters entering at the top of your head, smoothly flowing down *through* your body, from head to toes. Set your intent for the flow to gently, quietly, but effectively erode away the causes and results of past injuries or disease. (Don't worry about taking "more than your share" of these waters. You have an inborn right to all you want and need.) See the water coming down just as quickly or as slowly as seems right. If you start to receive ideas or insights into the causes of various problems, don't let them interfere with the process. File the ideas away for later examination if need be, but hold your attention on the waters flowing smoothly down through your body. . *During* the meditation, *do* the meditation. Do it as long as seems appropriate, and stop when you feel like stopping. Much more important than how long you do this exercise is how often you do it. The more often, the better, even if it's only a minute or two at a time.

2) The *"Blue Flame Of Consciousness meditation.* As a part of the River of Life and Health meditation, or alone, envision a blue flame within your forehead, above the eyes. A flame of any kind has been a symbol of consciousness for many years, and a blue flame (as opposed to yellow) burns clean. Let this symbol remind you that there is another part of yourself beyond time and space, benignly observing you living your life, wishing you well, rooting you on. A continual (or even occasional) reminder may serve to keep your ego, with its fears and desires, from blinding you to the fact that you are more than what is obvious.

3) Last and perhaps most powerful, your *Control Panel visualization.* What this amounts to is recreating your life to your own design, on an on-going basis. If there's anything more powerful than that, I can't think what it is. (I owe this technique to psychic Ingo Swann. I once heard him respond to a question as to how he would go about changing some trait in himself by saying, "I'd just change my control panel." I immediately knew what he meant.)

Think of it this way. You are the captain of your own ship, but you don't necessarily run the engine room or personally do everything required to keep the ship operating. You have a crew for that. Well, they get their instructions by consulting the standing orders, and the control panel is how you post them. Visualize a bank of switches, either circular rheostats or slide-switches. Create one for any quality in your life that you wish to increase or decrease. (You can add switches at any time, of course.) Give the slide switch a minimum and maximum range, or have either end of the scale represent opposing characteristics. Set the switches—by your *intent*—where you want them. You have just told your crew what you want. It's really that simple.

Staying Connected

These simple techniques to help you live your life amount to directing your life by staying connected. That's easy. What *isn't* so easy is remembering to stay connected. Here are four ways to stay connected. Use what feels right to you.

1) If you can *pray*, pray, routinely, matter-of-factly, with faith that your prayer is heard. Don't just ask for change, but be grateful for what you have. Don't think of yourself as a worm of a sinner, unworthy to be heard, but think of yourself as co-creator of your life. Don't beg, but confidently expect. And don't whine, but seek to understand. You are not alone, regardless how it sometimes feels.

2) If you can't pray (or even if you can), *meditate*. Quiet the mind and feel yourself a part of all of life. If trying to dismiss all thought leads only to distractions and wool-gathering, try holding your mind to one image, one idea, something like, "I am part of all life, visible and invisible, and I will not be led out into the wilderness and abandoned there." Meditation lessens your fear and your sense of isolation, and if it did nothing else, it would be well worthwhile.

3) If you can't pray or meditate (or even if you can), you can always *visualize*. Don't be misled by the connotations of the

word. *"Visualizing" does not mean seeing pictures!* It isn't like you close your eyes and a movie starts showing. Visualizing is holding in your mind an image, or an idea, or a feeling. *Visualizing is imagining.* Everybody on earth does it. You do it every time you remember something, or daydream about something.

4) Finally, if you can't pray or meditate or visualize (or even if you can), you can always *relax*. Sitting quietly, or lying down—comfortable enough to relax, but not so comfortable as to fall asleep—close your eyes. Sometimes you can hear your pulse, thumping in your ears. Even if you can't, you can always concentrate on your breathing. In either case, first fall into the rhythm and then consciously, calmly, imagine it slowing down. Yes, you can affect your heartbeat, just as you can affect your breathing. Slow it down, and just for a few minutes calmly relax. You do have the right to relax! Anything that is stressing you will still be there when you finish, but for these few minutes this is *your* time. Relax. Then develop the habit of reminding yourself every so often to remember what relaxation feels like.

So there you have all you need. Reprogramming, to overcome the past. Access to guidance, to steer a course. Visualizations, to aim you toward a future.

Conclusion

"Every time a civilization reaches its moment of crisis, it is capable of creating some higher type of man. Its successful response to the crisis depends upon the creation of a higher type of man. Not necessarily the Nietzschean Superman, but some type of man with broader consciousness and a deeper sense of purpose than ever before. Civilization cannot continue in its present muddling, short-sighted way, producing better and better refrigerators, wider and wider cinema screens, and steadily draining men of all sense of a life of the spirit. The Outsider is nature's attempt to counterbalance the death of purpose. The challenge is immediate, and demands a response from every one of us who is capable of understanding it."
—Colin Wilson, *Religion and The Rebel*

The guys upstairs made it plain more than once. In their view, life is not so much about *learning* as it is about *choosing*. Life presents us with challenges, we choose among them, and life presents us with more challenges. Gradually, as the process continues, we create ourselves. And this is the gift we bring to the other side when we are finished with this life: the self we have created.

The materialist nightmare that says that life is meaning-less is just that, a nightmare only. For centuries now, a certain kind of person has felt that only the muddleheaded or the timid could believe in an afterlife. The self-described hardheaded realists "knew" that this world was all there is, and that how we fill our time is a matter of personal choice without consequences to ourselves or others. How well that worldview has worked out, you can see by looking around you.

If that worldview had been factually correct, then the disastrous social consequences that followed from it would be something we would have to accept as the price of preferring truth to pretense or fairytale. But it is not.

You are not alone, and you are not what you think you are. We are all part of one being, just as mystics have always asserted. Our lives here on earth are the invaluable and irreplaceable prelude to our eternal lives, just as religions have always maintained. Life on the other side of the veil that separates the physical and nonphysical—regardless how difficult we find it to envision—is closely connected to this physical life, and depends upon our choices, just as fairytales, for instance, have always said. The world is a struggle between opposing values, a local-ized battlefield, so to speak, in a far vaster conflict, again, just as religions have long maintained. However, although this is true, it is equally true, as Carl Jung pointed out, that good cannot exist without evil, that any polarity must include opposites, and that therefore for us to be whole we must recognize our own shadow sides.

In his old age, Jung was asked if the world could be pre-served, rather than being destroyed by a nuclear holocaust. His answer was that it could be preserved, if enough individuals would do the necessary work on themselves. He may have been right, he may have been wrong, but in either case this is the considered opinion of the greatest psychologist of our time. His opinion was founded upon his decades of first- and second-hand experience with the intricacies of the human psyche. It would be rash to assume that he didn't know what he was talking about.

Given Jung's words and given the worldview sketched above by the guys upstairs, there is no excuse whatever to continue to believe that your life is trivial or meaningless. Just the opposite. When our souls separate from our bodies, it is not the end of us, but, in a sense, the beginning. Nothing is ever lost.

About the Author

Frank DeMarco was co-founder of Hampton Roads Publishing Company, Inc., and for 16 years was chief editor. He is the author of three previous non-fiction books (*Muddy Tracks; Chasing Smallwood,* and *The Sphere and the Hologram*), and two novels (*Messenger: A Sequel to Lost Horizon* and *Babe in the Woods*). He also conducts workshops on communicating with guidance, and writes a monthly column for the on-line magazine, *The Meta Arts*. His past and current thinking may be found on his blog, *I of My Own Knowledge….,* on "Everyday explorations into our Extraordinary Potential." Visit him at www.hologrambooks.com.

Related Titles

If you enjoyed *The Cosmic Internet*, you
may also enjoy other Rainbow Ridge books.

Conversations with Jesus:
An Intimate Journey
by Alexis Eldridge

Dialogue with the Devil:
Enlightenment for the Unwilling
by Yves Patak

The Divine Mother Speaks:
The Healing of the Human Heart
by Rashmi Khilnani

Difficult People:
A Gateway to Enlightenment
by Lisette Larkins

When Do I See God:
Finding the Path to Heaven
by Jeff Ianniello

Rainbow Ridge Books publishes spiritual
and metaphysical titles, and is distributed by Square
One Publishers in Garden City Park, New York.

To contact authors and editors, peruse our titles, and
see submission guidelines, please visit our website at:

www.rainbowridgebooks.com.

For orders and catalogs, please call toll-free:
(877) 900-BOOK.